WILLIAM JOHN WILLS

WILLIAM JOHN WILLS

PIONEER OF THE AUSTRALIAN OUTBACK

JOHN VAN DER KISTE

Cover illustrations, front: William John Wills; *back*: Burke, Wills and King in the desert, from an engraving by Nicholas Chevalier, 1868.

First published 2011

The History Press
The Mill, Brimscombe Port
Stroud, Gloucestershire, GL5 2QG
www.thehistorypress.co.uk

British Library Cataloguing in Publication Data.
A catalogue record for this book is available from the British Library.

ISBN 978 0 7524 5855 7

Typesetting and origination by The History Press
Printed in Great Britain

Contents

Acknowledgements

My thanks are due to Mike Wills and other members of the family in England and Australia, and to Dave Phoenix of the Burke and Wills website. Between them they have been a mine of information as well as lending several photographs for reproduction, and cheerfully answering many questions in the course of my researches. Wendy Major, Ruth Westall and Brian Lewis were kind enough to show me round St Lawrence Chapel Heritage Centre, Ashburton, the site of Wills' former school, in addition to providing me with illustrations and the benefit of their expertise. Both Barrington Weekes of Totnes Image Bank and Rural Archive and Paul Spiring assisted with additional material, as did Russ Parkin with some of the photography. As ever I am eternally grateful to my wife Kim, who read the manuscript and made several useful suggestions for improvement and assisted with the photography. My final acknowledgements are to my editors Simon Hamlet, Abbie Wood and Lindsey Smith at The History Press, for their encouragement and hard work in seeing the book through to publication.

BURKE AND WILLS EXPEDITION
1860 – 1861

GULF
OF
CARPENTARIA

CAMP
119

Albert R.   Flinders R.

CLONCURRY

S E L W Y N   R A N G E S

BIRDSVILLE

Victoria R.

Lake
Eyre   DIG TREE   BRISBANE

BULLOO

COOPER'S   KORLIATTO
CREEK

TOROWOTO

Darling R.

Murray R.   MENINDEE
Murrumbidgee R.

ADELAIDE   BALRANALD

SWAN HILL   SYDNEY

CASTLEMAINE

BENDIGO

BALLARAT   MELBOURNE

ROUTE

Introduction

Among the annals of British explorers during the last 200 years, no name perhaps ranks higher than that of Robert Falcon Scott, leader of the ill-fated expedition to the Antarctic in 1911–12, who perished with his companions. By curious coincidence, another man born in South Devon in the nineteenth century was similarly destined to play a major role in important exploration. Like Scott, he (and his leader) came tantalisingly near to success just fifty years earlier, but a combination of errors and severe misfortune meant that he too perished on the journey.

His name was William John Wills, a tragic hero of his time. Initially appointed as the surveyor, he was later promoted to second-in-command, and is rightly remembered as the first person to navigate a route across Australia from Melbourne in the south, to the Gulf of Carpentaria on the north coast. Again, like Scott, it is ironic that Wills might not be remembered so well by successive generations if he had returned from the expedition alive and well.

The story of the 'Burke and Wills' expedition – or as the people of Totnes declared at a public meeting after his fate was known, the 'Wills and Burke' expedition – has been told by several authors, notably Alan Moorehead, Tim Bonyhady and Sarah Murgatroyd, whose invaluable studies are cited in the bibliography. Posterity has been grateful to Wills for his conscientiously kept journal of the expedition, without which only meagre records and recollections of the venture would exist. However, despite this, until now no individual biography has sought to portray the short life of Wills in full. It is the aim of this book to redress the balance.

The four seasons of the year are different in Britain and Australia. As a rule, summer in Australia is considered to last from December to February, autumn from March to May, winter from June to August and spring from September to November. The Victorian exploring expedition, which departed from Melbourne in August 1860, therefore set off in winter.

1

A Devon Childhood

The surname Wills comes from the Anglo-Saxon *atte wille*, meaning 'living by the water'. In the tax returns for 1332, there were twenty-eight men named Wills listed as living in south Devon, each one a potential source of a different Wills lineage. Most of them were born and lived in southeast Devon, in or near the towns and villages of Totnes, Ilsington, Lustleigh, Bovey Tracey and Bickington. They chose their wives from the neighbouring areas and sometimes there were marriages between cousins in order to merge their holdings of land. In due course there were more male members of the family than farms available, and some either adopted other occupations or immigrated to America, Canada or Australia.

By the beginning of the nineteenth century, therefore, the Wills family had been farming in Devon for several generations. John Wills, born in 1760, had farms firstly at Smallacombe, Dawlish, then at Compton Barton, near Marldon – close to Compton Castle and Torquay. In 1787 he married Sally Rendell at Combe-in-Teignhead, and between 1788 and 1804 they had nine children. The eldest, Sarah, married Commander Henry Le Vesconte of Jersey and they settled in Canada in the 1830s. Their son, also called Henry, was a member of the polar expedition led by Sir John Franklin in 1845 to search for the Northwest Passage, and perished with the rest of his men when their ship became icebound in the Canadian Arctic. Over a century later, his bones were found and buried at Greenwich. Exploration, it seems, was in the family's blood.

The youngest of their nine children, William, was born at Ilsington, according to different sources in 1800 or 1804. After studying medicine he married Sarah Mary Elizabeth Calley in 1830, and they settled at No 3 The Plains, in Totnes. It was here he established his own practice and their seven children were born. A daughter, Elizabeth Rose, who was born on 18 September 1831 and died in 1852, was the first. She was followed by William John on 5 January 1834; the short-lived Thomas was born in 1835 but died a year later; another son who took the same first name, Thomas James, was born in 1837; a third son, Charles Henry, was born on 23 September 1839; and finally two more daughters, Elizabeth Margaret, born on 30 January 1843, and Hannah, born on 24 March 1845.

It was their second child and eldest son who ensured that the family name would be long remembered. As a child William John showed early signs of great intelligence, not to say precociousness, and according to his father he could speak and walk without help before his first birthday. His younger brothers teasingly called him 'Old Jack', or 'Gentleman Jack', because of his serious outlook on life, while his father called him 'Gentleman John', or 'my Royal Boy'. He was sometimes known in the family, and later at school, as John. However, he is generally known to posterity as William John Wills, and throughout this biography he will be referred to as William or Wills.

According to his father, 'his lively disposition gave ample employment to his nurses, though I cannot remember that he ever worried one, through peevishness or a fractious temper'. When he began to talk distinctly, 'he evinced an aptitude to name things after his own fancy; and I may fairly say, that he was never a child in the common acceptation of the term, as he gave early indications of diligence and discretion scarcely compatible with the helplessness and simplicity of such tender years'. Fathers are not necessarily the most objective judges of their own children, particularly if they are uncommonly gifted, and these reminiscences were written not long after his beloved son's untimely death. A touch of rose-tinted parental exaggeration may therefore be taken for granted. Nevertheless, there is evidence that throughout his short life William John Wills was an extremely intelligent, painstaking young man and this portrait of him in childhood, gilded though it may be, is certainly credible.

When he was aged about 3 or 4, one of their nearby friends, a Mr Benthall, asked for parental permission to take the lad for a walk in his garden.

William had just begun attending a school for small children in the district, kept by an elderly lady. Less than an hour later, Mr Benthall returned to ask if William had come home. Nobody had noticed him, and his parents were concerned lest he might have fallen down a well in the garden. With dread in their hearts they went to have a look, but were soon satisfied that nothing of the kind could have happened. Nevertheless, the boy still failed to return, and they became increasingly worried until Sarah Wills suggested he might have made his way back to the school. When they went to look, she was proved right. The boy, so devoted to his studies, was sitting at his desk with a book in his hand. While Mr Benthall had been speaking to the gardener he had managed to give him the slip, returning unnoticed to the schoolroom on the opposite side of the square.

Another characteristic incident took place not long afterwards. Dr Wills' brother, who lived overseas, came to stay with them in Devon. One day he needed to visit Plymouth and Devonport, and the doctor arranged to take his brother there in a gig. The latter asked Sarah if his little nephew could accompany them; she gave her permission and they spent the night at the Royal Hotel in Devonport, where the landlady and servants were very impressed by the little boy. Next morning the brothers kept separate early business appointments elsewhere, having arranged the previous day that they would sit down to breakfast at ten o'clock. When they returned to do so, young William was missing. They thought that somebody else must have taken him under their wing, but none of the household had seen any sign of him for about an hour. After searching high and low for twenty minutes or so, they found him standing at the window of a nautical instrument maker's shop, about ten doors down the street from the inn, on the same side of the road, gazing in riveted attention at the fascinating display before him. The proprietor of the shop told Dr Wills that he had noticed him for more than an hour in the same place, examining the instruments with the eye of a connoisseur, as if he completely understood them. William's thirst for scientific knowledge had proved rather greater than his appetite for breakfast.

During his early years William contracted remittent fever and was so ill that at one point the family feared they might lose him. As he lay in bed, slowly recovering but still very weak, their elderly servant Anne Winter, who had faithfully nursed him and stayed by his side for much of the time, was particularly concerned lest he might have suffered some mental damage as a result. She was delighted when a neighbour's tame magpie flew in through the window one day and hopped across William's bed, causing him to roar

13

with laughter. Even so, recalled the doctor, following the illness the appearance of his features altered slightly, giving him a more striking resemblance to the family on his mother's side than on that of his father. He was also left with a slight speech impediment, which stayed with him for life.

For a time he was considered not strong enough to go to school and he stayed at home, where he received tuition from his father. They discovered in each other a kindred spirit:

> Instructing him was no task; his natural diligence relieved me from all trouble in fixing his attention. We were both fond of history. From what I recollect, he took more interest in that of Rome than of Greece or England. Virgil and Pope were his favourite poets. He was very earnest with his mother in studying the principles of the Christian religion. More than once my wife remarked, 'that boy astonishes me by the shrewdness with which he puts questions on different points of doctrine'. In his readings with me he was never satisfied with bare statements unaccompanied by reasons. He was always for arguing the matter before taking either side. One question, when very young, he would again and again recur to, as a matter on which the truth should be elicited. This was a saying of our old servant … when she broke either glass or earthenware: that 'it was good for trade'. His ideas of political economy would not permit him to allow that this axiom was a sound one for the benefit of the state; and on this point, I think, Adam Smith and Malthus would scarcely disagree.

As the family had already seen, he was evidently an old head on young shoulders. His father considered that although he might be childlike in his habits and manners, William was never a child in intellect. He could be trusted with anything, and Dr Wills was sometimes taken to task by his contemporaries for letting the boy handle a gun when he was only 11 years old. His first practice was on some rooks which he brought down with a steady hand from a rookery in the grounds at their country home.

Though he might not think twice about the ethics of killing wild birds for sport, William was devoted to animals. He once saw a man beating a horse savagely, and the sight disgusted him. As the family did not have a dog, he used to take their cat to accompany him in the fields and hunt in the hedgerows. When his father went for long walks in the countryside, he took William with him, and found he was always asking for information on one subject or another. As soon as he showed an interest in astronomy, his father immediately began to teach him the names and positions of the main constellations, all about the revolutions of the earth on its axis, and the fixity of the polar star. The doctor was sure that they were the first people to notice a comet in 1845, 'which was only a short time visible here, having a south declination, and which we afterwards knew to have been a fine object in the Southern hemisphere'.

It was no surprise that this extraordinarily clever infant soon became something of a child prodigy. Instead of going out to play with other children, William preferred to spend his spare time helping out at his father's medical practice. In those days the doctor was often also a dentist and midwife, and living in a small town with the countryside and a large rural community close by involved considerable travel. Dr Wills was therefore very grateful for such a valuable assistant who always seemed very cautious and conscientious in everything he undertook.

From an early age William was also an enthusiastic reader, often to be found engrossed in a book. To his favourite poets he soon added the eighteenth-century man of letters Philip Stanhope, Earl of Chesterfield. Yet his first choice always remained Alexander Pope, and throughout his life he would often quote selected lines from Pope's work in letters to his parents.

In 1845 the family left Totnes and moved about 6 miles north, finding a new home in the village of Ipplepen. It was claimed that Dr Wills employed a coachman by the name of Henry Mathews Baskerville, a man who later showed the writer Arthur Conan Doyle around parts of Dartmoor when he was staying at Princetown in 1901 – inspiring him to write *The Hound of the Baskervilles*. However, this particular Baskerville was not born until 1871 and the dates, therefore, do not fit the story. He was named after a maternal uncle, Henry Mathews, who had lived at Ipplepen and was described in the census returns as a retired coachman. This may well have been the man who served Dr Wills.

By now, the home tuition of William John Wills with his father was coming to an end. In the autumn of 1845, when he was aged 11, William was enrolled at St Andrews Grammar School, Ashburton, for the next stage of his education. It was part of St Lawrence Chapel, a chantry chapel, where the children of the town and surrounding areas sang the mass in return for an education from the resident priest. Bishop Walter Stapledon had presented the chapel to the town in 1314 when he was Bishop of Exeter and Lord of the Manor of Ashburton. One of the first grammar schools in England run by the Church for the education of boys aged between 11 and 16, it retained this status until its closure due to falling numbers at the end of the summer term in 1938. Other distinguished pupils included three worthies born in the town, namely: John Dunning, later 1st Baron Ashburton, the eighteenth-century lawyer and politician who became solicitor-general; William Gifford, the author, critic and editor of the *Quarterly Review*; and John Ireland, Dean of Westminster, who carried the crown at the coronations of George IV in 1821 and of William IV ten years later. It held its chief endowments from Gifford and Dr Ireland.

Dr Wills was reluctant to let William go away to school, but he had to agree with friends that to keep the boy isolated at home would only hold back his development; 'a public seminary where he could mix with other boys was an advantage, even though he might not learn more'. It had the additional advantage that Mr J. Brown Paige, MA, whom Dr Wills had known for some time and whom he regarded as very well qualified, had just been appointed headmaster. William went there as a boarder, staying in one of the dormitories in the headmaster's residence, Ireland House, in East Street. Dr Wills returned in low spirits after taking his son and leaving him there for the first time. While he had four other surviving children, he was honest enough to admit that his first son was undoubtedly his favourite. Now he deeply missed the boy's constant companionship, which he said helped him to acquire 'more knowledge than he imparted'.

Surprisingly, in view of his love of learning, William did not make remarkable progress once he had started at school. However, his father did not admit to disappointment just because William did not return home at the end of every half-year with the head prize. Indeed, all he had was his 'six months' bill', and:

a letter commending his steady diligence and uniform propriety of conduct. In *viva voce* examinations he had scarcely an equal chance with one of inferior intellect who might be quicker in expression; for besides the trifling hesitation of speech I have already noticed, he would have been ashamed to give a wrong answer from eagerness. A remark of Mr Page [sic], his tutor, confirmed me in my own previous impression on this point. 'It vexes me,' he said, 'that John does not take a top prize, for I see by his countenance that he understands as much, if not more, than any boy in my school; yet from want of readiness in answering he allows very inferior lads to win the tickets from him.' On the whole, I think he derived much benefit from Ashburton; for besides his scholastic improvement he became an adept at the usual games, and a social favourite out of school hours.

Apart from the speech impediment, this tutor's report suggests that he was diffident and a slow thinker. Yet appearances are often deceptive, and beneath the apparently pedestrian exterior lay an extremely shrewd brain.

At the age of 16 William finished school, leaving behind him one small lasting memorial. It had long been a tradition at such institutions for pupils to carve their names on the benches or desks. On the first bench on the right as one enters the schoolroom, the boldly incised letters 'WILLS' can still be clearly seen to this day.

Upon leaving Ashburton Grammar, on 30 May 1850, Wills was articled to his father's surgical practice. Dr Wills had just taken on a partner at Ipplepen, Henry Manly, in order to introduce and hand over to him his practice in the town. As they lived in a country area, where there was no chemist or dispensary, young William readily took to his duties, which in addition to extracting teeth and other routine operations, now included distributing medicines and appliances directed for his father's patients.

In 1851 his father took him to London for the first time to visit the Great Exhibition. It came as no surprise to the doctor that the 17-year-old should be fascinated by all the scientific instruments and mechanical inventions; he could hardly spend too long in studying them. When they left the exhibition to see something of the rest of the city, if his father ever showed any signs of losing his way in the tangled web of unfamiliar streets, William would instantly put him right. How, he asked, had the boy acquired all this knowledge? 'On the second day,' William answered, 'when you were out, I took the map and studied it for two hours, so that now I am well versed in it.'

It became evident to his father that William had 'some instinctive power in matters like these, such as horses and carrier-pigeons possess'. When they went to Windsor Castle, young William was told that it was considered a major feat to climb the statue of King George III which stood at the end of the Long Walk in the Great Park. He immediately accepted it as a challenge, and managed to do so in very little time. At Hampton Court he demonstrated his remarkable sense of direction by solving the maze in about ten minutes. Most of those with whom he came into contact were convinced that he was an unusually meticulous, talented young man who would surely have a bright future ahead of him.

In the spring of 1852 his father took him to London again, to study medicine. At this time there was no class dedicated specifically to human anatomy, so young William had to study that branch of science by visiting the museum at Guy's Hospital. Dr Wills had been a student there himself, and he introduced his son to his old teacher, Charles Aston King, through whom he obtained permission to attend. William witnessed surgical operations at the theatres of several hospitals on a more or less daily basis, but the only class he entered was that of practical chemistry, which he studied under Dr John Stenhouse at the Medical School of St Bartholomew's Hospital, London.

Towards the end of the course, Dr Wills asked Dr Stenhouse if his son was showing any particular talent in the subject. In response, Stenhouse begged him not to take away one of the most promising pupils he had ever had, assuring Dr Wills that on the strength of what he had seen so far, within two years, 'in practical chemistry, he will be second to few in England'. At the time Dr Stenhouse had some responsibility for analysing different articles of food sold in the shops, and in the course of his work he always found his young pupil's suggestions and comments helpful.

While he was a student William stayed in a house near the hospital. The elderly couple and servant who looked after him were impressed when he showed them what he had discovered of the tricks practised by street traders. Whether he actually apprehended any wrongdoers or was responsible for any arrests, history does not relate, but his temporary landlord said that the young man would undoubtedly distinguish himself if he was to find work with the detective department of the London police.

When William returned to Devon later that year, he brought with him a testimonial from Dr Stenhouse, signed on 1 September 1852:

> I have much pleasure in certifying that Mr. W. J. Wills attended a course of practical chemistry at this medical school during the summer season of 1852. He obtained considerable proficiency, and invariably distinguished himself by great propriety of conduct.

If he had stayed in England and sought a career in London, William would have surely risen to the top of his profession, and in a very short time. Opportunities in Devon would have been rather more limited, and had he remained there, he would probably have found little scope for his talents beyond following in his father's footsteps as a country doctor. In addition, the quiet, conscientious youth of 18 was already yearning for adventure beyond any which a steady life in his home land could ever offer him.

2

Early Life in Australia

The circumstances which would ensure the immortality of the name of William John Wills in history, and also, sadly, his untimely death, were gradually unfolding. In 1851 gold was discovered in Victoria, a state in the far south-east of Australia, firstly near Ballarat, then at Bendigo, and subsequently at several other sites. The ensuing gold rush, one of the largest the world had ever seen, led to a huge influx of migrants, particularly from Britain, Ireland, Germany and China. Until then, Australia had been known primarily in Britain as the main destination for transported convicts, a practice which officially ended only in 1840. Now the discovery of the precious metal 'changed the popular conception of Australia from a place of social sewage to a land of untold opportunity'.[1]

Victoria grew rapidly in economic power as a result. Within ten years the population had increased sevenfold from 76,000 to 540,000, and the state produced an estimated 20 million ounces of gold, about one-third of the world's output. There was inevitably a darker side to this success story, for disease flourished in cramped, unsanitary conditions on the gold fields, producing epidemics such as the outbreak of typhoid at Buckland Valley in 1854 which claimed over 1,000 lives. Yet in the nineteenth century, casualties on such a scale were regarded as part of the regrettable price of progress. Victoria revelled in its new-found wealth, and its capital Melbourne grew rapidly to become Australia's largest city and the second largest of the British Empire. It was the start of a boom which lasted forty years, and the arrival of large numbers of educated gold seekers from abroad contributed to the rapid growth of schools, churches, learned societies, libraries and art galleries. The University of Melbourne was founded in 1855 and the State Library of Victoria in 1856, while the Philosophical Institute of Victoria was founded in 1854 and became the Royal Society of Victoria after receiving a royal charter in 1859.

Among those in England seeking a new life on the other side of the world was the sculptor Thomas Woolner, one of the Pre-Raphaelite artists, whose journey was to be immortalised in Ford Madox Brown's painting *The last of England*, though he returned home not long afterwards. The Wills family from Devon stayed rather longer. Dr Wills bought a share in the Melbourne Gold Mining Company in 1852 and made plans to leave for Australia with his two eldest sons, 18-year-old William and 15-year-old Thomas. They would travel on board the *Ballarat*, with Dr Wills as medical attendant. Sarah was not readily reconciled to him going so far away, and did not want them all to travel on the same ship, partly as she did not wish them all to leave her and go to the other end of the world at once, and partly because if the worst should happen and the vessel was wrecked, she would lose them all at a stroke. William realised how upset she was, although she kept her feelings and her views largely to herself. 'I see my mother is grieving,' he told his father, 'although she says nothing, at our all leaving her together. Let Tom and me go alone. I will pledge myself to take care of him.'[2] Dr Wills accordingly cancelled their passage together, and secured an alternative voyage for his sons that autumn.

While the boys were preparing for the journey, Dr Wills found that William had obtained 'a large quantity of stuff rolled up like balls of black rope-yarn'. It turned out to be pigtail tobacco. 'In the name of goodness, are you going to chew or smoke all the way to Australia?' he asked. William smiled and replied, 'This is to make friends with the sailors. I intend to learn something about a ship by the time we reach our destination.'[3]

Promising faithfully to keep their parents informed as to their adventures on the other side of the world, the boys took their farewell of England as they sailed from Bayard's Cove, Dartmouth, on 1 October 1852 aboard the *Janet Mitchell*. William was fascinated by everything he saw on the journey. He kept a daily log of the weather and sea conditions, learnt the name and use of every rope, the arts of splicing and reefing and of every part of the ship's tackle from stem to stern. He discovered how to set the sails, and during a storm he was the first to go aloft, lending a hand in taking in topsails. At the same time he also acquired skills; he could catch a 5ft shark, which he would cut in slices, then add butter, pepper and flour to bake it like a hake.

After a ninety-five-day passage they dropped anchor at Williamstown, Melbourne, on 3 January 1853 with 197 fellow passengers, and found themselves accommodation at the Immigrants' Home in South Melbourne.

Before long the brothers decided they did not care for the city, particularly what they saw as its lawlessness. Intent on getting out of the area, they looked for work elsewhere, and in February they found employment as shepherds at a property owned by the Royal Bank Company on the Edward River near Deniliquin, for £30 per annum. On 12 February 1853 William wrote to their father, a letter which may be quoted in detail:

> We are very comfortable, in a hut by ourselves, about four miles from the station. We have between thirteen and fourteen hundred rams, by far the smallest and easiest flock, under our charge. We take the hut-keeping and shepherding in turns. The hut is a very nice one, built of split wood, and roofed with bark. It is close beside a pleasant creek or river, where there are plenty of fish and ducks. I assure you we make ourselves quite snug here. One of us rises almost as soon as it is light, gets some breakfast, and starts off with the sheep; lets them feed about until ten o'clock, then brings them slowly home, where they lie down until four; after that, they go out again until sunset. The other stays within to clean up the hut and prepare the meals. We can kill a sheep when we like. The worst part serves for the dogs, of which we have three – a sheep dog, and two kangaroo dogs. The latter are good, and keep off the native curs at night. The sheep dog was the only one the former owner had last year, to watch a flock of five thousand sheep.
>
> But you will want to hear something of Melbourne and how we came here. The first discovery we made after we got into port was, that we had to take ourselves and things ashore at our own expense … It was four shillings each by steamer to Melbourne, and thirty shillings per ton for goods. It cost us about 2 pounds altogether. At Melbourne we found everything very dear; no lodgings to be had, every place full. At length we were offered lodgings at sixty shillings a week, to be paid in advance, and twenty-five persons sleeping in the same room; but we preferred the Immigrant's Home, a government affair, just fitted up for the accommodation of new-comers, where you pay one shilling a night, and find yourself. You must not stay more than ten days.

We got there on Friday and remained until the Saturday week following. We then obtained this situation, and started on the same afternoon. Twenty-three of us came up together. Drays were provided to carry our luggage, but we ourselves had to walk. We were three weeks on the journey, through the bush, sleeping, of course, in the open air.

Melbourne is situated ... on the Yarra Yarra, which has not nearly so large a bed as the Dart, although more navigable. It is narrow but very deep, and so far resembles a canal rather than a river. The town, or city, as they call it, is situated low, but laid out on a good scale. The streets are very wide, and I think when filled with houses it will be a fine place; but what spoils the appearance now is, the number of wooden buildings they are throwing up, as they cannot get workmen for others. When we were there, butter was from two shillings and fourpence to three shillings per pound, bread fourpence, milk eightpence per pint, vegetables enormous, butcher's meat and sugar, as at home. Fruit very dear; a shilling would not purchase as much as a penny in England. Beer and porter, one shilling per pint in Melbourne, but from two shillings to two and sixpence here. The town of Melbourne is all on one side of the river, but on the opposite bank is Canvas Town, connected with Melbourne by a good bridge of one arch. Canvas Town takes its name from being entirely composed of tents, except a few wooden erections, such as a public-house, and the Immigrant's Home, where we had lodged. I do not like Melbourne in its present state. You are not safe out after sundown, and in a short time you will not be safe during the day. There were some men taken out of the river drowned, suspected to have been murdered, and several attempts at robbery, while we were there. I sold my box of chemicals, after taking out what I wanted, for 4 pounds, and the soda-water apparatus for 2 pounds 5 shillings. I also sold some books that we could not carry, but got nothing for them. Scientific works do not take. The people who buy everything here are the gold-diggers, and they want story books. A person I know brought out 100 pounds worth of more serious reading, and sold the lot for 16 pounds.

We started from Melbourne on a Saturday, with the drays, eight bullocks to each, laden entirely with the luggage of the party, twenty-three in number. We made only five or six miles that afternoon, and slept under some gum trees. Our clothes were nearly saturated with dew; but as we advanced farther inland, the dews decreased, and in a night or two there was no sign of them. The land for a few miles is dry and sandy, but improves as you proceed ... There was no scarcity of water, except for the first fifteen miles, after leaving Melbourne. We enjoyed the journey much, and shot many birds, which constituted our principal food. Ducks abound in the creeks, and up this way there are fine white cockatoos, which are good eating, and about the size of a small fowl. There is also a bird very plentiful here which they call a magpie. It is somewhat the colour of our magpie, but larger, and without the long tail; easily shot and eatable, and feeds, I believe, much like our wood-pigeons. The pigeon here is a beautiful bird, of a delicate bronze colour, tinged with pink about the neck, and the wings marked with green and purple. They are tame, and nicer eating than those at home. Where we are, we have abundance of food; plenty of mutton, and we can get a duck, pigeon, or cockatoo whenever we like, almost without going out of sight of our hut, besides a good supply of fish in the river; Murray cod, which in the Murray are said sometimes to weigh eighty pounds, but in our creeks generally run from two to twelve; also a kind of mussel, and a fish like a lobster, not quite so large, but good eating.

Everyone who comes out does a very foolish thing in bringing such a quantity of clothes that he never wants. All you require, even in Melbourne, is a blue shirt, a pair of duck trousers, a straw hat or wide-awake, and what they call a jumper here. It is a kind of outside shirt, made of plaid, or anything you please, reaching just below the hips, and fastened round the waist with a belt … It ought to be made with a good-sized collar, and open at the breast, like a waistcoat, only to button at the neck, if required. We brought out the wrong sort of straw hat, as they are only fit for summer, but we sold all but two. One I made six shillings of, but the cabbage-tree hat is worth a pound. No one should bring out more than he can carry on his back, except it be to sell. Boots and shoes are at a great price, but they should be thick and strong. Wages are very high for butchers, carpenters, and bakers. A butcher's boy can get 3 pounds a week, with board and lodging. Bullock-drivers get the same. Innkeepers are making fortunes. I know a public-house, not larger than the Two Mile Oak [a small public house between Totnes and Newton Abbot], that cleared 500 pounds in three months, so it was reported. Sydney, I hear, is as cheap to live in as London. As to the diggings, I cannot say much about them. I have seen many who have made money there, and many who have lost it again. It is generally spent as fast as it is got. I hope we shall send you some specimens of gold dust soon.

Subsequent letters followed at regular intervals, all in a similarly cheerful vein. William told in detail of his management in his shepherd's life in the bush, of how he converted legs of mutton into excellent hams by pickling and smoking them, and how he also obtained preserves of melons, by sowing seeds which were quick to ripen and produce new fruit. While he found the flies and ants a persistent nuisance, the heat was quite bearable, especially when tempered by a constant gentle breeze.

The brothers soon fell in love with the landscape, and were fascinated by all the different species of animals and birds:

> You cannot think how glad I am that you let us come out here. If you had only let us come out without a shilling it would have been worth more than a thousand pounds in England, one is so free. This is a beautiful country, the more I see of it, the more I like it.

Like most European settlers at that time, William maintained a rather superior attitude towards the indigenous population of Australia; he had 'a low opinion of their intellectual powers, and thought little could be done with them'. Nevertheless, his future experiences, when he was largely dependent on their bounty for survival, would lead him to revise his opinion for the better.

That summer William found he could add veterinary skills to his talents when he performed a successful operation on a sheep. While shearing one of his animals, a farm worker had accidentally run the point of his shears into the neck of one, and pierced the carotid artery. The quick-thinking Wills, who generally carried a small pocket case of instruments with him wherever he went, immediately set to work on the wounded animal and stitched up the wound. It made a full recovery.

Soon afterwards, Dr Wills fulfilled his promise to follow the boys out to Australia. He obtained an appointment as superintendent surgeon of a government emigrant ship, and he arrived there in August 1853. It took him over two months of asking around before he discovered where his sons were. Once he found out, he bought a horse and made the journey in four days, with one day's rest. On reaching Deniliquin he went to the hotel to refresh before he was reunited with his sons.

While travelling, Dr Wills was warned to be on his guard against 'stickings up', or robberies on the road, and thefts at the hotel. One travelling gentleman who had arrived there just before him had taken his saddle off his horse, put it under the veranda, and then led the horse to a nearby paddock. He then returned to find the saddle had gone. Assuming one of the staff had taken it, he put his bridle down in the same place, went to have a drink with the landlord, and asked him if he had got the saddle. The landlord denied taking it, but the traveller insisted he had left it under the veranda, where he had just put the bridle as well. Both men went back to the same spot – to find that now the bridle was also missing. These stolen goods would have probably fetched about £20.

When he went to the station Dr Wills found an aborigine who was happy to act as his guide. Both men rode on their horses to a dry creek where the guide pointed to a dry path; he followed the path for about 3 miles until he found himself in front of the hut. William and Thomas were naturally over-joyed to see him again. A few days later the brothers disinterred their money which they had buried at the foot of a gum tree on a nearby hill, intending to give £100 as a present to their mother as soon as they had the chance. They then left Deniliquin on horseback for Melbourne. On their journey they paid a visit to the Bendigo diggings, where William demonstrated his skill by using his compass to lead them through a trackless bush, resulting in a shortcut of several miles.

Father and sons returned to Melbourne before moving to Ballarat, where Dr Wills set up a surgery among the wooden shacks and trenches. He was among those who attended the injured in the Eureka Rebellion of gold-diggers at Ballarat in December 1854, in which demands by the miners – including the right to vote, purchase land, and achieve a reduction in the price of the miner's license – resulted in a pitched battle with the police and military personnel. About thirty were killed and many more wounded. William spent the next couple of years working simultaneously as a digger on the goldfields, as assistant surgeon in his father's practice, looking after patients in the senior man's absence, and running an office in which he analysed specimens of gold and quartz. For two years he toiled hard. For leisure he took brisk walks, or went swimming in Port Phillip Bay; only rarely did he allow himself such diversions as a visit to the opera. Spending his evenings in public houses, drinking more than was good for him – let alone witnessing the brawling of others who had already done so – were not for him. Alcohol was the ruin of many a promising life in Australia among those with too little to do. Another man who recognised as much was the British missionary Revd R. W. Vanderkiste, who had spent several days in New South Wales in 1854 and wrote of his experiences about nine years later, noting that 'strong drink is a frightful bane to our colonies, and eats fearfully into the very vitals of our prosperity'.[4]

Wills' letters occasionally alluded to enjoyment of dancing, but not with female companions, and he may have been rather shy or reserved in their company. He wrote at great length on science, education and literature, and somewhat sceptically on religion. Barely a letter to his siblings went back to England that did not encourage them, in a manner which verged on hectoring, to improve themselves. The picture which emerges is of an extremely conscientious, self-driven young man, maybe even a little priggish, perhaps lacking in social skills and a sense of humour. He set himself high standards, and expected the same of others, especially in his own family.

Even so, his father felt that William was constantly pining to be back in the bush, where he could spend as much time as he wanted studying the flora, fauna and stars, preferably on his own. The 'busy haunts of men' did not appeal to William at all. Time and again his conversation turned to the interior, and his hope that one day he would be able to undertake a journey to the Gulf of Carpentaria on the north coast. It was inevitable that he would seize any opportunity to be part of an expedition that was being discussed at the time. His heart was not in following a medical career, as he said 'it was not clear and defined in practice', and he was convinced that medical men were less valued for their real worth and scientific expertise 'than for their tact in winning confidence through the credulity of the public'. To William it was like the fortunes of certain people in the goldfields, where the greatest impostors would obtain credit for a time before making their fortune and disappearing as swiftly as they had arrived.

In January 1855 William John Wills went to stay with William Skene at the Kanawalla Station, Hensley Park, on the River Wannon near Hamilton. Skene, a Scot, was devoted to his bagpipes and would often walk around outside playing them, or as Wills and his father put it: 'waking the echoes of the wilderness ... the noble fern trees and the fine black cockatoos.' All the time William continued his practice in surgery, but apparently made no charge to his patients on the grounds that he was not licensed as a doctor and thus had no right to demand money from them.

Three months later William believed that the moment he had been waiting for had come. He was still thirsting for adventure when his father wrote to tell him that he had heard of an expedition being planned by an American, Dr Catherwood. On receiving the letter he immediately packed his blankets and kit. He wrote to his mother on 22 April 1855 of his hopes of joining the party, which was:

> about to explore the interior of the country, which you appear to have such
> a dread of. It seems uncertain whether they will go at all. As to what you say
> about people being starved to death in the bush, no doubt it would be rather

disagreeable. But when you talk of being killed in battle, I am almost ashamed
to read it. If every one had such ideas we should have no one going to sea
for fear of being drowned; no travellers by railway for fear the engine should
burst; and all would live in the open air for fear of the houses falling in.

Determined to be part of the expedition, William walked from Kanawalla
Station, where he was staying, to Ballarat, a distance of about 100 miles.
But he never caught up with Dr Catherwood. Instead, having obtained
several hundred pounds in public subscriptions to finance the venture,
Catherwood had revealed himself as a confidence trickster, absconded with
the lot, and was never heard of again.

Putting it down, philosophically, to experience, Wills returned to work
in Ballarat at the end of April. Never idle, he also promptly set to work
completing a small wooden annexe to his father's house, building the sides
and shingling the roof. The result proved perfectly weatherproof, and stood
there for several years until it had to be removed when the street was wid-
ened. Having thus proved his building skills, William decided he wanted
to study surveying. He was appointed as an amateur to the office of John
Hamlet Taylor, acting district surveyor in the Ballarat survey office on Sturt
Street. He spent several months learning trigonometry, Euclid drawing and
geometry by day, and working hard in his own room to complete his studies
by night. When Dr Wills got up in the morning, he would often find his son
sitting at his desk as he had left him the previous night, loath to push any
work or problem aside until he had completed or solved it.

In the summer Wills began studying field-surveying. He started his practical experience at Glendaruel, near Tourello, working under the supervision
of Frederick John Byerly, assistant surveyor, for a salary of £150 per annum
plus board and lodging. Most young men of his age in Ballarat passed their
leisure time on the town, but William, ever anxious to better himself, preferred to read textbooks on mathematics or astronomy, putting any spare
money towards new scientific instruments and books of astronomical
tables. In the course of his studies he gradually became convinced that it
was science, not God, which explained or would explain the universe and
everything that happened within it. His letters home accordingly became
rather more sanctimonious, even dogmatic in the beliefs he expressed.

A diligent student himself, he was equally keen to do what he could
to encourage the education of his siblings from afar. Another letter to his
mother, written from Glendaruel on 20 August 1856, accompanied a copy

of Bonwick's *Geography of Australia*, warning that they must not look upon it as infallible as he had already found a mistake, possibly a misprint with regard to the location of a particular lake. At the same time William advised his mother to encourage her children to learn drawing – not merely sketching, but perspective drawing with scale and compasses, as it was 'a very nice amusement, and may some day be found extremely useful'. They would be well advised to acquire an understanding of Euclid, mathematics in general and algebra in particular. These, he said, are 'the best studies young people can undertake, for they are the only things we can depend on as true (of course I leave the Bible out of the question). Christian and Heathen, Mahometan and Mormon, no matter what their religious faith may be, agree in mathematics, if in nothing else.'

In February 1857 William was working at Bullarook Creek Camp, and in March he had a couple of weeks surveying at Kingower near Inglewood. Later that year he was promoted to foreman, was placed in charge of a field party, and his salary was increased to £185 per annum. His father was keen to make him a gift of a set of surveying instruments, and he asked William to send a list and an order to whom he regarded as the best London stockist for his needs. William accordingly did so on 20 March 1857, with a request that they should be supplied by Messrs Troughton and Sims, Fleet Street, at their 'most reasonable prices'. Among the items he asked for were:

One four-inch theodolite, best construction [£21] ... one of Troughton's best reflecting circles, eight-inch radius, divided on silver [£23] ... one prismatic compass, three-and-a-half inch, with silver ring [£5 5s] ... one six-inch semicircular protractor, with Vernier [£3 3s] ... one glass plane artificial horizon, ordnance pattern [£4 4s] ... one brass rolling parallel ruler, two feet long, must not weigh less than five pounds ... four sixty feet land chains ... one small compact case of good sector-jointed, drawing instruments with ivory parallel ruler [£3 3s] ... Two Nautical Almanacs, 1858 and 1859.

Lastly, Wills asked for a set of leather straps for a theodolite, circle, and prismatic compass and a priced catalogue of instruments. These requests were accompanied by careful instructions as to how the instruments were to be packed; in his experience they were vulnerable to the box becoming warped inwards or outwards, so that it would either press too much on the instruments, or even worse, leave them too much space so they would shake about whenever the box was carried. As a result the screws would loosen, the glasses would fall out of the telescopes, and the instruments would become unfit for use. He suggested that this could be avoided by having the parts of the box which touched any instrument well padded with elastic materials, and for the lot to be supported on steel strings, strong enough to keep it firmly in place, and with sufficient play to allow the box to warp without injury to the contents. Above all, he asked that they should be insured to the full value.

The instruments were speedily despatched. Wills was delighted with them, and for the rest of his short life they were his pride and joy. Before he left on his expedition in 1860, he asked his father to pass all his remaining items to Mr Byerly in the event of his not returning afterwards.

Senior officers in the Surveying Department were very impressed by the young man's progress in his subject. One of them told his father admiringly that he thought it wonderful William had 'mastered this business almost by his own exertions, while I have cost my father nearly a thousand pounds in England, under first-rate teachers, and am glad to go to him for information on many points'. When Dr Wills thanked Byerly for having ably instructed his son, he was told, 'Don't thank me; I really believe he has taught me quite as much as I have taught him'.

Wills' regular queries and suggestions inspired his father to investigate other aspects of the science. He had acquired that instinctive ability of finding out for himself the use of any instrument put into his hands, and how it should best be used. With this went a ready eye for any faults it might have. When a colleague who had made some errors in his surveys asked him to have a look at his instruments, doubtless with a view to discovering where he was going wrong, Wills picked one up and examined it. 'If you work with this,' he said, 'you will find many errors.' 'That is why I asked you,' the man answered, 'I have been surveying with it, and have committed nothing but mistakes.'

If Wills had one regret at this stage of his career, it was that he had not worked harder at maths during his schooldays. He often told his father that the hours he had spent exclusively learning the Classics were 'time thrown away'. His father was amused to recall that the boy had initially shown little enthusiasm for mathematics, apart from algebra, which he always enjoyed.

From April to June 1858 William John Wills could be found surveying at St Arnaud. On 10 April he wrote separate letters to his brother Charley, who was planning to work in the bank at Totnes, and to his mother. After reminding his brother a little sternly that he had not written to him since they had come out to Australia, he wrote:

I wish you could be here, instead of working for 40 or 50 pounds a year at home, out of which you can save very little. Here you might be getting at least 100 pounds, and nothing to find yourself but clothes. But it will not do for you to come until the Doctor goes home. I want you to write and tell me if you have any taste for any particular profession, and if you have been making good use of your spare time, in reading useful works. You should remember never to waste a minute; always be doing something. Try and find out what things you have most taste for, as they are what you should study most; but get a general knowledge of all the sciences. Whatever else you learn, don't forget mathematics and the sciences more immediately deduced from them, (at the head of which stands astronomy,) if you have any love of truth – and if you have not, you have none of your mother's blood in you. Mathematics are the foundation of all truth as regards practical science in this world; they are the only things that can be demonstrably proved; no one can dispute them. In geology, chemistry, and even in astronomy, there is more or less a mere matter of opinion …

Wills then mentioned that with the letter he was enclosing the sum of £3, which was to be spent on a few particular improving books which he had priced for them. The list included *Chambers's Mathematics*, Parts 1 and 2, and *Chambers's Mathematical Tables*; the current edition of *A Nautical Almanac* for next year; and Dr Lardner's *Museum of Science and Art* in six double volumes, 'one of the best books that has ever been written. It includes a general knowledge of nearly everything you can think of, and will be as useful to Bessy and Hannah as to you.' Not content with sending this reading list, he told them that they would need somebody to help them by explaining various points in the mathematics and algebra if they expected to make good progress:

After getting the books I have mentioned, you may spend the balance in any others you please, but remember, they must be scientific ones. If you write to Walton and Maberley, they will send you a catalogue of books published by them, in which you will find descriptions of nearly all that I have mentioned and plenty of others. You can order those you want direct from them, or get them through a local stationer. I expect you to acquire some practice at printing, and ornamental writing, in the Bank. If you have a steady hand, you should exercise yourself at it as much as possible, and learn mechanical drawing at the same time. Draftsmen get well paid out here, and are greatly in demand. Being able to print neatly and evenly is the main point: all the rest is easily learned. My hand is very unsteady, as you may see by my writing; I do not think I shall ever be able to write a decent hand. One other piece of advice I must give you before I shut up; that is, never try to show off your knowledge, especially in scientific matters. It is a sin that certain persons we know have been guilty of. The first step is to learn your own ignorance, and if ever you feel inclined to make a display, you may be sure that you have as yet learned nothing.

It is tempting to wonder how William's siblings in England received such letters from their elder brother in Australia. Did they faithfully obey his instructions, or did they resent his zeal in the efforts he was making to direct their education and development from afar, and simply spend the money on whatever they wanted instead?

In his letter to his mother on the same day, William made a few revealing observations on his own personality, as well as a slightly pompous comment on those around him in Australia, and a suggestion that the rest of the family should consider following him out there:

> From what I can judge of this dear son of yours he is not likely, I think, to do anything very rashly; and as for getting married, he will not be in a position to think of that for several years; and if ever he does, I hope it will be to some one at least equal to himself in education. Give my love to Bessy and Hannah. I do not think it would do them any harm to write a letter sometimes … Does it ever enter your head that it would be a good thing for all of you to come out here in a few years, when the girls have finished their education? This country is undergoing great changes for the better. Now the rush to the diggings is over, people are beginning to live like civilized human beings. In a few years everything will be as settled as in England, and we shall be able to live much cheaper.

Early in the summer, after a petty disagreement between Byerly and Mr Duffy, the Chief Commissioner of Land and Works, Wills left his employment and went to Melbourne for a short time. On 6 June he wrote again to his father:

> What you say about this world I do not quite agree with; I think it a very good world, and only requires a person to be reasonable in his expectations, and not to trust too much to others. It appears to be almost equally divided

into three principal classes – honest fools, foolish rogues, and honest rational beings. Some may add another class, but there are so few belonging to it – scarcely one in ten thousand – that I think it should be ranked amongst the phenomena of nature. I mean, the successful rogues – men who do things neatly, and escape being found out. The first and second are often useful to each other; the third benefit by the first and second, inasmuch as they learn by their experience, without paying for it themselves.

At the same time, he cautioned his father against being led into temptation by ill-considered financial speculations. Here indeed was an old head on young shoulders. Later he went on to say he was planning to change his 'station', and ended by discussing Nelly, a small colt he had hand-reared. She went in and out of the tent 'as if she had been born in it', and shook hands (or paws) with everyone.

Returning to Ballarat in July, Wills took occasional contracts surveying for Clement Hodgkinson, the deputy surveyor general, before moving back to Melbourne in August, where he took lodgings for four months with a Mrs E. Henderson at Dorcas Street. On 15 August he wrote to his mother, apologising for not having written more recently yet pointing out that he had not heard from her for several months, and delivering an implicit rebuke in pointing out that his siblings, 'Charley and the girls', did not write at all:

I have just left the bush and am living, for the present, in town. The change is pleasant, after being so long in the bush. Melbourne is wonderfully altered since I last saw it. There are some very fair buildings in it now, and things are a little cheaper than they used to be. I am, of course, living in lodgings, and am fortunate in getting into a comfortable house; a private family with no other lodgers, and Mrs H. takes almost as much care of me as you would. It is quite strange, and at the same time amusing to me, to see her anxiety about my eating, drinking, catching cold, and all that sort of thing, as I have been so long unaccustomed to these little attentions. I am sure if some of you who have never been away from home were to see how we live in the bush, you would not expect us to survive more than a few weeks, and yet it does us no harm whatever. I passed through Ballarat on my way down, and spent a few days with my father. He was looking better than he used to be, very healthy, and not so stout. It is astonishing how little he eats, and yet is always complaining of having eaten too much. I expect it will be the same with me.

I have as good an appetite as ever, but I can live on much less food than other people can. I hope Charley has the books I told him to get.

In November William obtained a temporary post on the recommendation of Charles Whybrow Ligar, surveyor-general at the magnetic observatory at Flagstaff Hill. Three months later one of the observatory assistants, John Walter Osborne, transferred from the observatory to become a photo-lithographer in the Survey Department of the Office of Crown Lands and Survey. Wills was appointed his successor and in March 1859, when his permanent appointment was confirmed, he moved into a room at the observatory and studied under its director, the government meteorologist Professor Georg von Neumayer.

Regarded by contemporaries as an incorrigible eccentric who 'worked like a madman', and if interrupted would look pointedly at his watch every five minutes, Neumayer was so obsessed with the idea of measuring the earth's magnetic fields that other people found it difficult to get him to talk about anything else. In William John Wills he found a kindred spirit. Wills thought he was the best man he had ever met, 'not the least selfish but a true lover of science'.[5]

Mr Ligar thought that Neumayer was likely to return to his native Germany before long, and he had the promising young Wills very much in mind as the next director if a replacement should be necessary. Wills was doubtless aware of these plans, and flattered that he should be considered for such a prestigious appointment at such a young age. Had this come to pass, he would probably have been able to stay there as long as he liked, working and living in comfort and drawing a reasonable salary for his work and expertise.

However, Wills was at times apprehensive that his employment might not continue indefinitely. There was always a danger that the local Parliament might decide to discontinue the grant for the observatory, and also the pos-sibility that Ligar might be overruled by others and someone might try to put another in his place, a prospect Wills did not presently relish: 'I hope I shall not have to go into the bush again,' he wrote to his father in December. 'I like Melbourne and my present occupation so much. But everything must be uncertain until after Christmas, as all depends on Parliament voting money for the Observatory. Should they not allow the necessary sum, I must return to surveying once more.'

Yet, as his father knew all too well, the sense of adventure which had brought him out to Australia made it unlikely that he would stay there long. Further opportunities were beckoning, perhaps sooner than he had anticipated. William had already been frustrated in his hopes of joining one expedition, and if such a chance was to come again, he would not be slow to respond. Mr Ellery, superintendent of the astronomical observatory at Williamstown, tried to persuade him to give up all thoughts of involvement with such a hazardous enterprise, pointing out to Wills, in vain, that he would earn twice as much salary and not be exposing himself to danger. However the quiet, ever industrious Wills knew his own mind, and would not be dissuaded.

On 16 March 1859 he wrote to his mother, mentioning that he was living in the observatory. He hoped that the younger members of the family were hard at their studies, and that in particular Charley would:

> take every opportunity of learning the things I mentioned in a letter to him some time ago, more especially mathematical drawing: and that I shall see in the next letter I receive from him that he has changed his mind as regards the profession he said he had a taste for. I wish he would find out for me whether there is a translation into English of Colonel Savage's Practical Astronomy. It is a Russian work, and the place to inquire is of some of the booksellers in London who confine themselves to foreign publications. I like my present employment more and more every day. My only trouble is the want of time. I hope you all find your time pass as easily as I do; if the girls do not, they may as well kill some of it by writing letters.

Another letter followed on 17 June:

> It was my intention to have sent you a stereoscopic photograph of your dear son by this mail; but owing to pressure of business I have been unable to get it done in time. I must therefore leave it until next month. I received a letter from Ballarat a day or two ago, containing one from you to my father; you say something in it about not hearing from me. I do not understand how that is, as I have been wonderfully regular lately, and have sent a letter every month to one of you. I am sorry to hear that the winter has been so mild, for I fear that may cause much damage from frost in the spring. We have had a considerable quantity of rain here already, which is a great benefit to the country generally, but makes it rather unpleasant in Melbourne. Wonderful improvements have been made in our public library lately. It is now really a splendid one; in fact there are very few better anywhere.

That same day he also wrote to his sister Bessy. True to form, he was still taking his mission to encourage his siblings in England to pursue their education very seriously. Did Charles, he asked her, obtain the maps of the stars which he told him to obtain some time earlier? If so, he ought to begin keeping a register of meteors in a copybook. A detailed example of 'meteor keeping' was added in the letter, as well as a request that 'If there is anything in the form that he does not understand he must ask me about it when he writes'. William finished the letter with another schoolmasterly instruction asking Bessy to let him know, next time she wrote to him, all about Charley and how he was spending his time. 'I am afraid that you little girls take him out walking too much, and make him read pretty stories instead of the books he ought to be studying.'

On 14 July William wrote again to his mother, on one of the rare occasions when events in the outside world had perturbed him. Late the previous month, the battle of Solferino had been fought between the French and Sardinian armies on one side, and the Austrian on the other. A decisive victory for the former, there were fears that it could escalate into war on a wider scale involving Britain and the Empire, if not the greater part of Europe. Although such fears were never realised, Wills was particularly concerned at the threat that French ambitions might pose to the power with whom she had recently fought alongside in the Crimean war:

> The news by the last mail has put us all in a state of excitement about our defences, in the event of England being involved in the continental war. Melbourne is badly situated in case of an invasion. There is at present not the least protection; and unless the home government sends us out two or three good war steamers, we shall most certainly get a good thrashing some day. The French have possession of the island of New Caledonia, which is not very far from here, and is a convenient place of rendezvous for them. I see by your letter to my father that you are rather afraid the French may invade England. For my part I believe they have more sense. It is the most hopeless thing they can attempt ... We have had some rather cold weather lately; that is, the thermometer has been below thirty-two degrees once or twice, which is cold for us.

Another letter to his mother followed on 6 August, with news of an accident on the coast which could so easily have been a tragedy:

You see I have sent you the News Letter for this month, with a long account of an unfortunate shipwreck that happened on the coast last month. It is a wonder how those passengers that were saved managed to exist so long without food. The only reasonable explanation that has been offered is, that as they were continually wet, from the sea breaking over them, a large quantity of moisture must have been absorbed by the skin, otherwise they could never have lived so long without fresh water. It must have been an awkward situation to be in. I fancy I would rather have been drowned at once; but it is not easy to judge how we should feel under the circumstances, unless we had tried it. As Pope says, 'Hope springs eternal in the human breast; man never is,' etc. (of course you know the rest). It strikes me that the height of happiness is, to hope everything and expect nothing, because you have all the satisfaction of hope, and if you get nothing you are not disappointed; but if you obtain what you want, you are agreeably surprised.

Letters from members of his family in England were a lifeline, and in return for his long, detailed epistles from Australia, Wills always hoped and expected the same in return. Another which he sent to his mother, dated 15 September, suggests that his family were not always forthcoming:

I was rather disappointed at not receiving a letter from any one by the last mail. I have not heard from my father since it arrived. I conclude he has not sent me your letters to him, thinking that I have received some myself. I suppose you are all glad that the war has ended so unexpectedly. It is to be hoped that the peace will be a permanent one, although people here generally appear to think that it will not prove so … Our winter is nearly over. Last night there was a festival held in honour of Alexander von Humboldt. It was unfortunately a very wet evening, which prevented a great many from attending who would otherwise have been there. I hope you are all in good health. It would have pleased you much to have seen the two splendid auroras, of which I have sent Charley a description. At one time it was light enough to read a newspaper out of doors, after the moon went down.

That same day he was writing a separate letter to Charley, much of it taken up with his excitement about the recent auroras, or natural light displays usually seen at night, some of it about books. Finally there was a reference to his hopes that the expedition he was looking forward to so much was about to become reality:

I send you by this mail two accounts of auroras, which we have had the pleasure of observing here ... You will perhaps be so good as to let me know by return of post whether anything of the kind was observed in England about the same time; and be careful to state the dates and hours, etc., as exactly as possible. You will find much, in the reports I have sent you, to object to, in the manner of expression and the words used; but you must make due allowance for their having been written by a German (Professor Neumayer). I have corrected some of the most prominent errors in the second. I wish you would look out for every description of auroras that may appear in the newspapers, as well as for the phenomena themselves. You might always cut out the paragraphs, and put them in a letter; and in the event of your seeing one yourself, you might write a description, being particular to note the time of the different phases as nearly as you can. By just taking this small amount of trouble you will be rendering a much greater service to the science of magnetism than you imagine; for one of the most important points is to establish or prove the existence of a simultaneity in the Northern and Southern Lights.

If you have yet obtained those books that I told you some time ago to get, you will find some elementary information on the subject in them ...

I suppose I shall hear by the next mail whether you have been able to obtain for me Savage's *Practical Astronomy*. I want to trouble you with another commission of the same kind, namely, to find out whether there is a translation from the German into English of Professor Carl Kreil's *Introduction to Magnetic Observations*, 2nd edition, Vienna, 1858. I fear you will have some trouble in getting this book for me, but it is of great importance that I should have it if possible. It may not be translated yet, but it certainly will be before long. Whenever you get any catalogues of scientific books from the publishers in London, you might send them to me in a letter; or if they are too bulky, you have only to put a strip of paper round, and send it as a book, without letter or writing ...

They have just succeeded in raising the two thousand pounds here, by subscription, that was wanted towards an exploration fund, for fitting out an expedition that will probably start for the interior of our continent next March. Camels have been sent for, to be used in places where horses cannot go. You would be astonished at the number of applications that are being made by people anxious to join the expedition. Nine-tenths of them would wish themselves home again before they had been out three months.

On 18 November Wills wrote to his mother again, advising her of his future plans:

We have had a very pleasant spring this year; not so many hot winds as usual … it is probable I shall be going up the country again in a few months, but that need not make any difference in the address of my letters, as Professor Neumayer will have the best opportunities of forwarding them to me. We have lately had a visit from Dr Hochstelter, a German professor, who came out in the Novara, an Austrian frigate, sent by the Austrian government to make a scientific tour round the world. Dr Hochstelter is a geologist, and has made a geological survey of New Zealand. He exhibited a few evenings ago at our philosophical institute a great number of maps which he has compiled during the short time he remained on the island, and stated many very interesting facts connected with them. From what he says, there is no place in the world, except Iceland, where boiling springs and geysers are so large and plentiful. The doctor goes home by this mail, and I suppose there will soon be a good work published by him, giving a description of all he has seen. I hope to visit New Zealand as soon as I return from the interior of this country.

The time was coming when he would be able to tell the family that there was every chance he would be chosen as one of the exploring party. At the same time he was aware that plans made one week could be completely altered the next, and he wrote on the subject as he had done to his father, with the reserve of the naturally cautious, until the matter was finally settled. He knew his mother and siblings would be anxious, and was keen to allay their fears. Yet it was difficult for him to conceal the excitement he felt at being so well placed to be selected for such an honour, and while he took the news seriously, he could not resist sharing such information with them.

By the same post, he wrote again to his sister:

It seems very likely that I shall be leaving Melbourne in March, to accompany the expedition for the exploration of the interior of this continent. It is calculated that we shall be away for about three years. It may be more, but it is not likely to be much less. It is not yet certain that I shall go. In fact, nothing is decided, not even who will be the leader; but I thought it would be as well to mention it to you now … But remember that my going away need not prevent your writing frequently; for it is likely there will be occasional means of communication with Melbourne for the first six months, and Professor Neumayer will take every opportunity of forwarding my letters. It is quite possible that I may not go, but it is more likely that I shall, as Professor N. is very anxious that I should, to make magnetic and meteorological observations, and he is on the Exploration Committee. If you have not been able to get the books I wrote for, for myself, you may as well leave them for the present.

Although he was still spending most of his time working or studying, he was now finding some welcome and much-needed relaxation in occasional visits to the theatre and opera. While science had always interested him far more than the fine arts, he had been 'indulging greatly in operas lately', and was now becoming something of an enthusiast:

I can understand that sort of music better than high-flown oratorios. The operatic company at the Theatre Royal is not first-rate, but as good as we can expect to have in a new colony like this. The pieces they have given are *Il Trovatore*, *Lucia di Lammermoor*, *Lucrezia Borgia* and *La Sonnambula*; the latter is a delightful one, but they cannot manage it satisfactorily, some of the songs are so difficult of execution.

One more of his letters from 1859, dated 16 December and written to his mother, is largely about the aurora:

Your remarks about the aurora borealis of the 12th of October were very interesting and valuable. We knew that there was an aurora there, but of course could not tell where it was visible. You little thought that while you were looking at the vibrations of those beautiful streamers of red and white light, I was watching sympathetic oscillations of little steel magnets, which we suspended by silk threads, in the underground magnetic house that you see the top of in the foreground of the picture. The magnets were sometimes moving about so rapidly that I could scarcely read them; and although the aurora was with you nearly at an end probably about ten o'clock, yet the magnets did not resume their normal position for nearly twenty-four hours after. You will see from this the advantage to be derived from noting all particulars with regard to these phenomena, whenever one has an opportunity of seeing them; for we must always consider the possibility of their not being visible at places where there are observatories, on account of clouds and other causes. One great point that has yet to be satisfactorily determined is, whether the effect on a magnet at one end of the world is simultaneous with the auroral discharge at the other; or whether a certain time is required for the effect to be communicated through the earth ... By-the-by, this day week is Christmas-day; and, if I am not mistaken, your birthday as well as Hannah's is near about this time. She must be thirteen or fourteen; but, upon my honour, I do not certainly know my own age. Was I born in January 1834 or 1835? I wish you all may have a merry Christmas and many returns of the same.

Over Christmas and the start of the New Year, Wills was busy preparing himself mentally for what would be the great adventure of his life. In twelve months, his circumstances would be irreparably changed.

3

Exploration

In 1857 the Exploration Committee was formed by the Philosophical Institute in Victoria, with the aim of investigating the practicability of fitting out an expedition which would travel across Australia from south to north. While interest in inland exploration was already strong in the neighbouring colonies of New South Wales and South Australia, in Victoria enthusiasm had so far appeared comparatively limited. An anonymous donation of £1,000 to the Fund Raising Committee of the Royal Society of Victoria for exploring the interior of the island continent of Australia, formerly New Holland, failed to attract much attention at first. It was not until 1860 – when the sum was increased to £2,000 by private subscriptions, with an additional £6,000 voted by the colonial legislature – that a sufficient £9,000 was raised so that the expedition could be assembled and members chosen.

Some of the Australian states were locked in rivalry for the honour of whose expedition would be the first to complete a crossing of the subcontinent. A telegraph line from England had recently reached India, and plans were being made to extend it to the major population centres of Australia, particularly New South Wales and Victoria. As a result, the mainland colonies were also competing for the honour of hosting the Australian terminus of the telegraph line. Western Australia and New South Wales were proposing the use of long undersea cables, while South Australia wanted to employ a slightly shorter cable, bringing it ashore at Top End – one of the two peninsulas on the northern coast – and run it overland to Adelaide in the south. The proposed route was remote and uninhabited by European settlers, and away from the main centres of population, while much of the land space was unknown territory, still waiting to be explored and mapped. Journeys of exploration needed to be made and the state of Victoria was determined to maintain her commercial pre-eminence. The formation of a committee to further such aims was the first step.

Next, the newly constituted body called for 'offers of interest' for a leader to come forward and take command of what it proposed to name the Victorian Exploring Expedition. Only two members of the committee, Ferdinand von Mueller and Wilhelm Blandowski, had had any previous experience in exploration and it was expected that one of them would be chosen as the leader, but due to factionalism among the other members both were consistently outvoted. Nevertheless, it appeared that as soon as somebody came forward and impressed everyone as a whole, the departure of the expedition would be only a matter of time. Wills intended to be part of it, and had high hopes that he would be selected as the official 'Surveyor and Astronomical Observer', a role for which he knew he was well qualified.

As he explained to his mother, if he was successful, it would be the moment he had been waiting for all his life. In a letter on 17 March 1860, William said she would be glad to learn the expedition was postponed as none of the candidates who had come forward were considered sufficiently qualified from a scientific point of view. Nevertheless, he was sure it would take place. Full of enthusiasm, he assured her that 'the actual danger' was nothing, 'and the positive advantages very great'. Although, he admitted, there was indeed an element of risk:

> You need not work yourself up to such a state of excitement at the bare idea of my going, but should rather rejoice that the opportunity presents itself. The actual danger is nothing, and the positive advantages very great … what avails your faith if you terrify yourself about such trifles? Were we born, think you, to be locked up in comfortable rooms, and never to incur the hazard of mishap? If things were at the worst, I trust I could meet death with as much resignation as others, even if it came tonight. I am often disgusted at hearing young people I know, declare that they are afraid of doing this or that, because they might be killed. Were I in their shoes I should be glad to hail the chance of departing this life fairly in the execution of an honourable duty.

Despite being preoccupied above all with his imminent great adventure, William still wrote regularly to the family at home. On 18 April in a long letter he took his sister Bessy to task as he had not heard anything from her during the month so far. He suggested that she might like to consider what a friend had just recommended to him, namely beginning a new letter at the start of each month, and add a small amount each day. In addition, there were other concerns on his mind about her way of life:

which may seriously affect your prosperity and happiness in this world. I fear that mamma is too much inclined to discourage your going into society. If so, with all due deference to my dear mother's experience and judgment, she has adopted a mistaken view. You will perhaps say, you do not care for society. So much the worse; that proves the evil of seclusion. I had the same ideas once, and greatly to my disadvantage in a general sense, although in one point they may have been beneficial, by making me devote more time to my studies. But I am doubtful even about that. At any rate, girls are differently situated. Having no need of deep scientific knowledge, their education is confined more to the ordinary things of the world, the study of the fine arts, and of the manners and dispositions of people. It is often asserted that women are much sharper than men in estimating character. Whether that be the case or not, is more than I can say, but I think it ought to be, because women have better opportunities and more leisure than we have for noticing little peculiarities and the natural expression of the features. Now, my advice would be, to go as much as you can into quiet, good society, and moderately into gay; not to make it the business of life, as some do, who care for little beyond frivolous amuse-ments, and that merely for the sake of killing time. But go to these places, even if you do not like them, as a duty you owe to yourself and others, even as you used to go to school, when you would rather have remained at home.

You should cultivate, as much as possible, the acquaintance of ladies from other parts of the country, especially of those who have travelled much. This is the best way of rubbing off provincialisms, etc. Perhaps you think you have none; nevertheless I shall be prepared for some whenever I have the felicity of seeing you. You cannot think how disagreeable the sound of the Devonshire drawl is to me now, and all people of the county that I meet have it more or less. You will, no doubt, wonder how I have become so changed, and what has induced me to adopt social views so different from those I formerly held. The fact is, that since I have been here, I have been thrown into every variety of companionship, from the highest to the lowest, from the educated gentleman and scholar to the uncultivated boor. The first effect was a disposition to admire the freedom and bluntness of the uncivilized; but more personal experience showed me the dark as well as the bright side, and brought out in their due prominence the advantages of the conventionalities of good society. While in the bush, this conviction only impressed itself partially, but a return to town extended and confirmed it. When we are in daily contact and intercourse with an immense number of persons, some of whom we like, while we dislike or feel indifferent about many others, we find a difficulty in avoiding one man's acquaintance without offending him, or of keeping another at a distance without an insult. It is not easy to treat your superiors with respect void of sycophancy, or to be friendly with those you prefer, and at the same time to steer clear of undue familiarity, adapting yourself to circumstances and persons, and, in fact, doing always the right thing at the proper time and in the best possible manner. I used to be rather proud of saying that it was necessary for strangers to know me for some time before they liked me. I am almost ashamed now not to have had sense enough to see that this arose from sheer awkwardness and stupidity on my part; from the absence of address, and a careless disregard of the rules of society, which necessarily induce a want of self-confidence, a bashful reserve, annoying to sensible people and certainly not compensated for by the possession of substantial acquirements, hidden, but not developed, and unavailable when wanted. I find now that I can get into the good graces of any one with whom I associate better in half an hour than I could have done in a week two years ago …

Since I wrote to you last, I have received some light on the subject of FAITH, which I was not at that time aware of. In a discussion with a gentleman on religious matters, some remarks were made upon faith and charity, which led to an analysis of the original Greek word used to express the former by St. Paul, which has been translated 'faith', and is generally accepted in the ordinary sense we attach to that word in English; namely, an implicit trust in what you are told, without question or doubt. But this friend of mine, who is a splendid Greek scholar, called my attention to the fact that the Greek word, for which we have no exact equivalent, means an openness to conviction, or a willingness to receive after proper proof; not a determination to believe without investigation. He also pointed out to me what I was less prepared to hear, that the charity spoken of does not mean, as I supposed it to express, conscientiousness, but love and good fellowship, in action and speech; in fact, more in accordance with the sense in which the word is commonly understood. This will show you the evil of coming to conclusions on insufficient data. Depend upon it, you must always hear both sides of a story before you can get at the truth.

I am going out to dinner this evening expressly to meet two of the finest girls in Melbourne. Some of my cautious friends say that I am running a great risk, and that I shall never recover from the effects. I cannot say that I feel much frightened. If anything serious should happen, and the consequences are not immediately fatal, I shall add a few lines to-morrow. Look sharp about photographs. I begin to suspect you are ashamed to show your face in this remote region.

Some of the letters published shortly after his death revealed that, while it might be exaggerating to call him a total atheist, he was anything but a devoted, unquestioning Christian. The lack of references to religion led some to consider that he was a sceptic, if not an infidel by Victorian standards, and several remarks might have perturbed other members of his family. Perhaps it is best to quote the comments of his father, without attempting to interpret them in any way, who wrote of William's 'admiration of a great and beneficent Creator, derived from the study of his works' and his 'distaste for sectarianism, and for a too slavish devotion to forms and conventionalities, whether in religious or social practice, fearing lest these extremes might savour of untruthfulness or hypocrisy'. William's mother, Dr Wills said, 'had instructed him early and zealously in the doctrines of Christianity, and prepared his mind for a conviction of their divine truth when he reached an age which would enable him to exercise his own judgment'. From childhood, William's enquiring mind had allowed him to take nothing for granted without investigation or questioning, a tendency which increased with maturity. Whenever he came across news of a fresh scientific discovery, or a newly improved mathematical or surgical instrument, he examined it carefully before adopting it.

As for his religious beliefs, said his father, William disliked 'any ostentatious display of religious sentiment and phraseology', and 'thought these matters better suited for inward communication between man and his Maker than for public exhibition on common matters'. It is not difficult to discover in William the mind of an agnostic, if not necessarily an atheist, and also a man who was reluctant to discuss such matters face to face with other people. One detects the personality of a conscientious, shy man, who would rather think deeply and commit his thoughts to paper. Among comparable contemporaries, one is reminded very much of Albert, Prince

Consort. Both men were destined to die within six months of each other; had they both been spared longer, and had a chance to meet, they might have discovered much in common with one another.

In May 1860 Dr Wills went to spend a few days in Melbourne, and found his son contented and happy, confident of being selected for the forthcoming expedition. William was lodging with a friend, and visited his father at his hotel, telling him that he wished to dine with him that day to introduce him to somebody whom he would surely like; 'his greatest fault is one you possess yourself, a turn for satire, which sometimes makes him enemies.' That same day he told the friend that his father had just arrived, and that evening when the friend wanted to invite William to a party, he replied with a smile, 'You forget that I have a wild young father to take care of'. This friend was probably Richard Birnie, son of a London police magistrate, a barrister who had studied at Cambridge and recently arrived in Australia.

It was Richard Birnie who wrote to the colonial secretary at Perth, endorsing Wills as a suitable person to be considered for the exploration:

He makes me happy beyond flattery by permitting me to think that I add something to his life. You cannot fail to like him. He is a thorough Englishman, self-relying and self-contained; a well-bred gentleman without a jot of effeminacy. Plucky as a mastiff, high-blooded as a racer, enterprising but reflective, cool, keen, and as composed as daring. Few men talk less; few by manner and conduct suggest more.

On 17 May William wrote to his mother of his father's recent arrival, asking her to excuse him a shorter letter than usual, as 'the Doctor has been in town for a few days lately, and of course seduced me into all sorts of wild habits. He is looking well, in good condition, but not so fat as he was two years ago.'

During the first few weeks of the year, several more people of varying ability and knowledge had applied for the post of leader of the expedition. By March the press was becoming increasingly scathing about the Exploration Committee's inability to choose anybody, to say nothing of rumours of drunkenness and in-fighting among the members. In the first week of March, it was reported from South Australia that John McDouall Stuart, who had already made three expeditions across Australia, had just set out on a fourth, his aim being to find the centre of Australia and continue to the north coast. Public opinion and the idea of rivalry from another state spurred the committee into action, and they reconsidered some of the men who had previously been recommended as leaders. The final catalyst, however, was the arrival at Melbourne in June of the camels which George Landells had been asked to provide for the expedition. At last there was one less excuse for not appointing a man in charge. Three candidates remained on the list, and the committee voted for Robert O'Hara Burke, a police superintendent who had been nominated earlier in the year.

Born in County Galway, Ireland, in February 1821, Robert O'Hara Burke was one of seven children, and the second of three sons. His parents were James Hardiman Burke, an officer in the British army 7th Royal Fusiliers, and Anne Louisa O'Hara, who married in 1817. His brothers were John Hardiman, who died in 1863; and James Thomas, a lieutenant in the Royal Engineers, who had been killed on 7 July 1854 at the battle of Giurgevo, the first British officer to die in action in the Crimean War. Robert O'Hara Burke entered the Royal Military Academy at Woolwich in May 1835, and completed his education in Belgium. In 1841 he joined the Austrian army, and was promoted to 1st lieutenant in 1847. A few months later he went absent without leave, possibly, it seems, because he had contracted a serious disease, thought to be respiratory. A more likely reason was a pressing need to escape his creditors, and at one point it seemed as if he would be court-martialled. After a preliminary inquiry established that he had contracted his debts 'in a light-minded manner' without any serious intent to deceive, he was permitted to resign.[1] Burke returned to Ireland and joined the Irish Constabulary. Immigrating to Australia in 1853, he joined the Victorian police force in Melbourne, initially as acting inspector in the parish of Jika Jika. Later that year he became a magistrate, was promoted to police inspector, then later to district inspector of the Ovens District. Inspired no doubt by the example of his brother James, he returned to England to fight in the Crimea, but hostilities ceased before he could enlist, and he was back in Victoria by December 1856. In November 1858 he was transferred to Castlemaine as police superintendent on a salary of £550 per annum.

Burke's appointment as leader of the Victorian Exploring Expedition was transparently a case of who, rather than what, he knew. He had no experience of exploration whatsoever and virtually no skills in bushcraft. The superintendent who recommended him gave the committee a character reference confirming that he was 'a most active man and very strong', as well as 'temperate in his habits', ambitious, determined and used to leadership. Burke had been a conscientious police chief and town prosecutor at Beechworth, north-east of Melbourne, and later in Castlemaine, and was very outgoing and well liked by his subordinates. Although he soon acquired a reputation as a keen disciplinarian, he was always ready to share jokes and stories with the locals, playing in the local orchestra and helping to establish a literary and scientific institute. His colleagues were ready to forgive him any shortcomings in efficiency and personal organisation, such as his lack of police uniform and a tendency to borrow suitable clothing from them whenever a local dignitary was expected in the area.

The reaction of the local press to Burke's appointment was lukewarm at best. The *Melbourne Herald* declared that the committee's selection process had been conducted throughout with 'strict impartiality', and if he was not the right man, the fault rested 'with fate'. More pointedly, the *Melbourne Weekly Age* ascribed his new position to 'an affair of cliquery', saying he had been selected without regard to his suitability. Most damning of all was the *Melbourner Deutsche Zeitung*, which reported all too accurately that he had no knowledge of science or the interior of Australia, and with him at the helm the expedition's prospects were poor. Another commentator feared that never before in the world's history had such an incompetent man 'entered upon an enterprise so great and responsible', and that lives would surely be lost.[2]

As regards the man whose destiny would be irrevocably linked with that of Burke, appearances could be deceptive. Wills' friend Richard Birnie described him not very flatteringly as having 'a light, clean, agile frame … and a handiness such as is often seen in a young girl'. Other colleagues realised he was steady, intelligent, dependable and abstemious, with a rare talent for surveying as well as a strong sense of duty. There was no suggestion that he was effeminate or precious, and during his years in Australia he had become adept at living in the wilderness. All things considered, Wills' merits complimented Burke's qualities admirably. Time would prove that Burke, who was superficially a more forceful and outgoing personality, was lamentably lacking in leadership skills.

George Landells, who had brought the camels to Australia, was made second-in-command, chosen for his communication skills with the Indian sepoys and his excellent way with looking after animals. Well aware of his importance, he produced a long list of conditions which he required the Exploration Committee to honour, including an annual salary of £600 and a guarantee that he alone would have responsibility for all matters relating to the treatment, loading and working of the camels, and to be fully responsible for their health. He also requested that the expedition should have 270 litres of rum for the camels for 'medicinal purposes'.[3] If these conditions were not satisfied, he would have nothing to do with the expedition. Such demands put the committee in a difficult position, as the salary he stipulated was £100 more than that of Burke, and for him to insist on having exclusive control of the camels was effectively undermining Burke's authority as expedition leader. Magnanimously, Burke supported Landells in his demands and graciously agreed to accept the lesser salary of £500. The committee conceded to Landells' requests; but while informing him that they could not grant him full authority over the camels, they told him in private that in all matters relating to their management, he could expect Burke to accept and follow his advice. It was an unsatisfactory compromise which implied that Burke would not be able to regard himself as fully in command, and provided potential for difficulties between both men in the future.

Having thus asserted his authority, Landells presented the expedition with a further problem. Camels had been used in desert exploration in other countries, but by 1859 only seven had been imported into Australia. In order to have the best animals available, he had been granted funds and given permission by the Victorian government to visit India and purchase twenty-four more. These arrived in Melbourne in June 1860. Six more were purchased from Cremorne Gardens, initially housed in the stables at Parliament House and later moved to Royal Park. However, in obtaining them Landells had spent double his budget, and he arrived back in Melbourne seven months later than planned. This delayed the start of the expedition, which should have coincided with the cool winter season. It was generally considered better to travel between April and September, when the temperature was more amenable and more water was available. This mattered little to Landells, who told the committee that his camels would cope well with any climate, as long as they were loaded lightly at the start of the expedition so they could conserve their strength for the more difficult desert terrain at a later stage. The committee took him at his word, and the inexperienced Burke did not know enough to be able to argue with him to the contrary.

With him Landells also brought six more men. John Drakeford had been appointed to work as camel handler and cook, while his assistant John King had recently been discharged from army service in India with chronic fever, and there was some doubt as to whether he had fully recovered. The other four, all camel handlers, were apparently Indian or Afghan.

Wills had submitted himself as surveyor, astronomical and meteorological observer, and as he had no rivals, his appointment was a formality. The committee made him third-in-command, and he was awarded a salary of £300 a year. Wills' intention was to make a genuine scientific examination of Australia during the journey, a mission which he shared with two other members of the expedition, the botanist and medical adviser Dr Hermann Beckler, and the artist and naturalist Ludwig Becker. Indeed, until Wills went into the Royal Society of Victoria's room to sign the contract – and was advised of the financial benefits by his father – he had been unaware that he would be offered any salary at all. The observatory's director, meteorologist Professor Neumayer, thought that Wills would not have time to pursue his scientific endeavours and plot the party's route at the same time, and recommended that Burke should take somebody else as a surveyor, but Burke said he had absolute confidence in Wills to discharge both tasks. Wills' main function would be the practical one of identifying their route across Australia, while studying the systematic registration of meteorology at their permanent camps, and recording magnetic observations whenever he could do so 'without interfering with the main object of the expedition'.[4]

On 17 June Wills wrote to his mother, apologising for the delay in replying to her last letter. He had only just received one from her dated 13 April and one from Bessy of about three days earlier; the mail had arrived much later than expected. In this letter he revealed that the question of religion was still very much on his mind:

Your endeavours to show that my remarks on religion were wrong, have tended to convince me more clearly that I was right, and that you, partially at least, misunderstood what I said. I did not charge you with being openly uncharitable or of plainly condemning any one; nor do I blame you for believing you are right. We all think we are right, or we should not believe as we do. But I do blame those who pronounce everybody wrong but themselves; for as far as we can judge, one may be as near the truth as another. How often we hear VERY religious people, compassionately remarking upon a neighbour's death: 'Ah, poor dear fellow, he was such a good sort of man! I hope and trust he died in the faith!' meaning, of course, their own peculiar tenets, and obliquely implying that, in spite of all his estimable qualities, they have great doubts of his salvation. For my part, I consider this as bad as the outspoken uncharitableness of bigots and persecutors in the olden days ...

But I must now come to the more precise point on which we differ – the meaning of a single expression … I allude to the word FAITH, which, as I was always taught to interpret it, appeared to my apprehension analogous to CREDULITY, or a blind belief without question; – an explanation which went against my conscience and conviction whenever it occurred to me from time to time. As I grew older I felt it to be wrong, although I was not sufficiently informed to explain it differently. What perplexed me was that St. Paul should advocate such a servile submission of the intellectual faculties which God has bestowed upon man; such an apparent degradation of the human mind to the level of the lower creation as to call upon us to lay aside our peculiar attributes of reason, common sense, and reflection, and to receive without inquiry any doctrine that may be offered to us. On this principle, we should be as likely to believe in the impostor as in the true saint, and having yielded up our birthright of judgment, become incapable of distinguishing between them. I have thought much on the subject with the assistance of better authorities and scholars than myself, and will now endeavour to explain what I consider St. Paul meant by FAITH, or rather by the Greek word *Piotis*, which has been so translated. After you have read my explanation, and carefully examined your own mind, will it be too much to expect an admission that of the three great elements of Christianity, faith, hope, and charity, you have hitherto had more of hope than of the other two? The Greek word used by St. Paul signifies something more than faith, or implicit belief, as many render it. It means a self-reliant confidence arising from conviction after investigation and study – the faith that Paley advocates when he says, 'He that never doubted never half believed'. It implies, in the first place, an unprejudiced mind, an openness to conviction, and a readiness to receive instruction; and then a desire to judge for ourselves. This must be followed by a patient investigation of evidence pro and con, an impartial summing up, and a conclusion fairly and confidently deduced. If we are thus convinced, then we have acquired faith – a real, unshakeable faith, for we have carefully examined the title deeds and know that they are sound. You will surely see that faith in this sense, and credulity, a belief without inquiry, are the very reverse of each other, and how much superior is the former to the latter. Credulity is a mere feather, liable to be blown about with every veering wind of doctrine. Faith, as St. Paul means it, is as firm as a castle on a rock, where the foundations have been carefully examined and tested, before the building was proceeded with.

In collateral evidence of what I have just said, I may instance the often-repeated injunction to accept things as little children; which cannot mean with the ignorance and helpless submission of infancy, but with minds free from bigotry, bias, or prejudice, like those of little children, and with an inclination, like them, to receive instruction. At what period of life do any of us learn so rapidly and eagerly as in childhood? We acquire new ideas every time we open our eyes; we are ever attracted by something we have not observed before; every moment adds to our knowledge. If you give a child something to eat it has not been accustomed to, does it swallow it at once without examination? Does it not rather look at, smell, feel, and then taste it? And if disagreeable, will it eat merely because the new food was given to it for that purpose? On the contrary, it is more inclined to reject the gift until influenced by your eating some yourself, or by other modes of persuasion. Let us then, in like manner, examine all that is offered to our belief, and test it by the faculties with which the great God has endowed us. These rare senses and powers of reasoning were given to be used freely, but not audaciously, to discover, not to pervert the truth … I think it is plain that St. Paul, while he calls upon us to believe, never intended that we should be passively credulous. Credulity was one of the most prominent engines of the Romish Church, but there was a trace of sense in their application of it. They taught that the ignorant and uneducated should have faith in the doctrines introduced to them by their betters, and those who had found time to investigate the matter; but some, in the present day, support the monstrous delusion that enlightened and well-trained intellects, the most glorious of all the earthly gifts of God, should bow to canting and illiterate fanaticism.

On 4 July a group of enthusiastic men hoping to take part in the expedition queued outside the headquarters of the Royal Society. About 700 had applied to join, some prepared to go for very little or even no wages at all, merely for the honour of being part of such a historical occasion. They had applied in writing, some with poorly scribbled notes, others with detailed accounts of equipment and supplies needed. Burke looked at them, then made an apparently arbitrary selection of those whom he believed had the right connections. At least two or three present had previously travelled on shorter expeditions through the Australian deserts and would have been ideally qualified, but they were passed over. Among those selected were William Brahe who had worked on the goldfields in Victoria, chosen mainly because his brother was a friend of Neumayer, and sailor Henry Creber, who was considered useful in case any inland seas should be discovered. Burke's other choices included four men whom he had met previously and regarded as friends: blacksmith William Patton and labourer Thomas McDonough whom he had known in Ireland, Patrick Langan whom he met in Castlemaine and Owen Cowan, another police officer, from Victoria. The fact that he was at pains to have people he knew suggests that he did not take the venture as seriously as he might have done, otherwise he would surely have been careful to select those better qualified by experience for such a potentially hazardous undertaking.

Several others were employed to fill subordinate roles. Charles Ferguson, a native of Ohio, was chosen as foreman to supervise the camp. After working in the Californian goldfields he had come to Victoria, taken part in a rebellion of miners against the cost of their licences, been arrested and managed to talk his way out of criminal charges. An adventurer by inclination, he became a cattle trader and horse breaker before founding an American-style steak restaurant in Ballarat because he thought the quality of Australian cuisine was dire. When it did poor business and closed within a few months, Ferguson had gone back to the goldfields in New South Wales. When he heard about the expedition, he talked his way into joining it, and was taken on as foreman at an annual salary of £200. Yet he had something of a roguish reputation, and one member of the committee warned Burke that he would probably 'have to shoot that man yet'.

On 25 July Wills wrote to his mother again. As he had probably realised, this would be his last letter to her before he set off, and he told her that they were due to begin the expedition within a few weeks. He had been advised that they did not expect to be staying away for as long as he had initially thought, and it might be as little as between twelve and eighteen months:

> I anticipate being able to send you a letter sometimes, as well as to receive yours to me, as they propose keeping up a communication with Cooper's Creek. Professor Neumayer will probably accompany us as far as the Darling River, taking an opportunity, at the same time, to prosecute the magnetic survey. This will make matters very pleasant, as well as being of great advantage to me in many respects. We shall be travelling through the country in the most favourable and pleasant season, when there is plenty of water, and everything fresh and green. It will take us about two months to get to Cooper's Creek. I do not give up my position in the Observatory, having obtained leave of absence for the time during which we may be engaged in the exploration. I am sorry I cannot give you more particulars respecting our projected tour, but you will hear enough about it by-and-by. I received a letter from my

father a day or two since, in which he speaks of coming down before I start. I do not expect to have time to go to Ballarat before we leave. I sent you by the last mail one or two small photographs of myself, and a locket for Bessy, which she asked me for some time ago.

While Burke apparently had a free hand in choosing his team, the Exploration Committee had the last word as regards timing. On 27 July they met to decide when the expedition should depart. Three months earlier, Sir Henry Barkly had announced that they proposed delaying until the following year, as to start before then would mean that winter would be almost over by the time the expedition reached the Darling River, and it would be wisest to explore the desert at the coolest time of the year. However, Burke was keen to start as soon as possible, citing 15 August as a suitable date – by then their provisions and equipment would probably be ready – and so 20 August was accordingly chosen as the date.

Yet by this date, no definite route had been agreed. Some committee members wanted to sail the camels halfway round Australia to Blunder Bay on the north-west coast, meaning the expedition would then cross the continent south to Melbourne. This idea was enthusiastically endorsed by Landells, who it seems had an eye on profits to be made from the voyage. Burke was persuaded to support the idea, and some of the committee agreed to do likewise. Chief Justice Sir William Stawell, one of the senior committee members, insisted that this resolution should be overturned however, and that the expedition would depart from Melbourne as planned.

News of these disagreements behind the scenes soon came to the notice of the local press, probably through disgruntled participants annoyed at not getting their way. Serious doubts were soon expressed about the competence of the committee and their wisdom in appointing Burke as leader. One journal, the *Melbourne Weekly Age*, reiterated the earlier suggestion that Burke's 'scientific attainments' were not equal to the task. If they were, the public ought to be reassured, otherwise they would 'protest against a piece of cliqueism in which the interests of the country are again sacrificed to please and serve the purposes of an unscrupulous and dangerous party'.[5] The implication was that the committee was prepared to send these men forth, possibly even sacrifice them to an undertaking which could end in disaster, all for the sake of possibly covering themselves with glory.

Perhaps it was fortunate that the two men who would ultimately lead the expedition did not have wives or children of their own to be anxious about their safety, even though one of them had an understandably protective father not far away. In none of his letters did Wills ever mention having a sweetheart. As a young man of 26, one would assume that as he had many years ahead of him, there would be plenty of time for him to settle down. Burke, 39 years old, a Protestant and also a bachelor, had become besotted with Julia Matthews, a Catholic actress half his age whom he had seen onstage in Sydney. He had apparently fallen in love with her from the front row of the theatre and then gone backstage afterwards in order to ask her to marry him. When her horrified mother learnt of this, she did her best to take her daughter out of harm's way and tried to find her an acting role in another theatre where Burke would be unable to find her.

That Wills was aware he might meet premature death, and was moreover willing to die if it was 'in the execution of an honourable duty', suggests a degree of fatalism, even resignation, on his part. Not long before they left, Burke told a friend that he had only one ambition, which was to do some deed before he died that would entitle him to have his name 'honourably inscribed on the page of history'.

By August, the great adventure had begun. William John Wills was full of optimism for the future, and looked forward to resuming his work at the observatory and being reunited with his family after it was all over. It was just as well for everybody concerned that none of them knew how very different the reality would be.

4

The Beginning of the Expedition

The Victorian Exploring Expedition, as it was officially designated, was scheduled to leave from Melbourne on Monday, 20 August 1860, at one o'clock in the afternoon. Nineteen men – five Englishmen, six Irishmen, four Indian sepoys, three Germans and an American – had prepared for a return journey of about 3,000 miles, perhaps more. With them they were taking twenty-six camels and twenty-three horses, plus six wagons full of equipment and stores. Apart from Wills, the Englishmen were John King and John Drakeford, both part of Landells' camel-handling team, whilst Charles Ferguson, the American, was the official foreman. Among the Germans was Ludwig Becker, the only member of the Royal Society who would be taking part in the expedition itself. He was a naturalist and artist whose job it would be to record the journey, particularly observing watercourses and mineral formations, and collect and sketch specimens of the mammals, birds, fish and fossils which they found on their way. The other was Dr Hermann Beckler, the medical officer and botanist who was entrusted with keeping a diary of the flora he observed, recording new species, collecting specimens and noting which plants were used by the aborigine tribes as food and medicine.

The supplies they had gathered to take with them included about 18,000lb of perishables; enough flour, sugar, tea, tobacco, meat, tinned coffee, preserved vegetables, lime juice, dried apples, raisins, currants and dates to last them for eighteen months to two years. They took about 400lb of medication for the camels and horses, and twelve water bottles. The animals' other needs were well catered for with twelve dandruff brushes, twelve curry combs, twelve water brushes, six mane combs, two clipping scissors and two clipping combs.[1] Furniture and amenities included a large bathtub, the rather questionable luxury of an oak and cedar table with two oak stools, flags, a Chinese gong and 45 yards of gossamer for fly veils.

The original plan was to take a number of additional camels which could be slaughtered for food en route, thus supplementing the dried meat rations already included in the stores. The meat rations, which required three wagons, slowed the expedition down considerably. Aside from the twenty-six camels which went with them, another six – two male camels, and two female camels with two young calves – were considered unsuitable for the journey and were left behind in Royal Park. Among the supplies were air bags to be lashed under the camels' jowls, to keep their heads clear should they need to swim across rivers or deep streams.

About 15,000 spectators gathered to see the expedition leave. The *Melbourne Herald* described the people who 'were to be seen along the dusty ways to the pleasant glades and umbrageous shade of the Royal Park', and the 'picturesque confusion' of men, horses, camels, drays and goods scattered among the tents, in the sheds, and around the whole area. There was a three-hour delay in their departure, experienced mainly because of Landells' fury when he was told that his camels all needed to carry 330lb more supplies than had been initially planned. Burke was particularly embarrassed and increasingly impatient as the city's dignitaries had been waiting for some time to bid them an official farewell. A speedy decision had to be made, and he hired two extra wagons for the supplies the camels could not carry. One 'cantankerous' camel, probably upset by the crowds and noise, broke free, ran through the startled crowd and had to be secured and brought back.

By around four o'clock all men, animals and wagons were at last assembled in an orderly fashion, and the mood among the crowds was increasingly enthusiastic despite the delay. A band of volunteer musicians struck up the tune *Cheer, boys, cheer*. One observer even likened it to a gathering which had come to see an army depart to fight the enemy, an analogy which some might have regarded as appropriate, especially when the unhappy outcome of the venture was known the following year. A path was cleared through the crowd, and a line formed with Burke on his grey pony at the head, while the Royal Society's Exploration Committee and a select group of invited visitors took up a position in front. The Mayor of Melbourne then mounted one of the drays, and addressing Burke told him he was 'fully aware that the grand assemblage, this day, while it has impeded your movements in starting, is at the same time a source of much gratification to you'. He assured him of the citizens' 'most sincere sympathy', and after wishing them Godspeed, called for three cheers for Burke, for Landells, and finally for the party itself.

Burke then addressed the crowds. On behalf of himself and the expedition, he thanked everyone who had come to see them off. To resounding cheers he said that no expedition had ever started under such favourable circumstances and the people, government and committee had done everything they could. It was now up to him and those who went with him to prove that they could justify the faith placed in them. His brave words were somewhat at odds with his remarks to close friends and associates that he intended to cross Australia or perish in the attempt.

If the outgoing Burke was happy to be the centre of attention, the same could not be said of his surveyor. It was noted that Wills avoided all revelry at the send-off, stubbornly refusing invitations to be interviewed or to have his photograph taken. Requests for the latter were met with a polite response that his father had an excellent likeness of him, from which anybody could copy, 'should it ever be worth while'. Wills was completely unmoved by the pomp, ceremony and almost carnival atmosphere going on around him. There were more pressing matters to be attended to, and he stayed inside his tent, wrapping his scientific instruments, placing them inside purpose-built mahogany boxes and ensuring everything was properly loaded. As surveyor he had full responsibility for a considerable amount of equipment and materials, and he took this just as seriously as the operations he had assisted his father with when little more than a boy. Among this equipment were nautical almanacs, a sextant, compass, theodolite, chronometer, barometer, thermometer, anemometer, telescope, specimen jars, several bottles of preserving fluid, sketchbooks and notebooks. Indeed, it was almost wholly thanks to his meticulous record-keeping in the latter that knowledge of the expedition could be handed down to future generations.

At half-past four the expedition finally left the park and the crowds slowly dispersed. Burke was followed by some of the assistants leading several pack horses on foot. Next came Landells and Becker, then two European assistants, all on camels, with one leading the ambulance camel and the other leading two beasts loaded with provisions. Sepoys on foot then led the remaining camels – four and five in hand, variously loaded – and this caravan was in turn followed by one mounted sepoy. A new wagon, heavily loaded, followed at a distance. It had been built especially for the expedition, constructed so that at short notice it could be taken off its wheels and used as a river punt to carry a heavy load high and dry on the water. Two or three hired wagons and another new one stayed in the park later still, nearly till dusk, in the charge of Wills and the foreman who were responsible for ensuring the careful packing of instruments and specimen cases. The hired wagons were to go only as far as Swan Hill, about 200 miles north-west of Melbourne. From the south gate of the park, the party went down behind the manure depot, and then on to the Sydney road.

After three hours the convoy reached Essendon, 7 miles away on the outskirts of Melbourne. As the camels arrived on the green in front of the church all the local horses bolted, repelled by the odour of these unfamiliar animals. The men then began to unpack and try to organise their camp. Dr Hermann Beckler was responsible for the management of the stores and he became quickly dismayed at Burke for having acquired a vast amount of equipment without much forethought, and for ordering the men to pack it at random so that nobody knew exactly where to find anything. It was one of the first indicators of Burke's haste and lack of proper organisation. Wills had packed his instruments, books and other materials with great care, but the others had not followed his example. Unaware that the chaos was mainly his fault, Burke marched round the camp telling everyone sharply that any disobedience or idleness would be firmly dealt with and all culprits would be nailed 'up by the ears to the nearest gum tree'.

As he did so, Dr Wills appeared, and there was an emotional parting between him and his son. The elder man then approached Burke and introduced himself, grasping his hand. 'If it were within my power,' he said, 'I would even now prevent his going.' After a pause, he added, 'If he knew what I am about to say, he would not, I think, be well pleased; but if you ever happen to want my son's advice or opinion, you must ask it, for he will not offer it unasked. No matter what course you may adopt, he will follow without remonstrance or murmur.'

'There is nothing you can say will raise him higher in my estimation than he stands at present,' was Burke's answer. 'I will do as you desire.'

That night the hopelessly infatuated Burke had one more mission. He had continued to worship Julia Matthews from afar, and secretly made a final return to the theatre to see her perform. Afterwards he went backstage again, presented Julia with his miniature portrait, and asked once more for her hand in marriage. He even offered to relinquish his place in the expedition, or at least postpone its departure, if she would give him her word there and then. Refusing to commit herself, Julia gave him a lock of her hair and agreed to reconsider when he returned. Burke placed the lock in a pouch around his neck and in a last will and testament, witnessed by two friends, he promised that in the event of his death he would leave her all his monies and other effects. He then returned discreetly to the camp at Essendon.

Australia was still in winter in August, and as the expedition moved north of Melbourne the bitter conditions worsened. Heavy rain and hailstones 'the size of billiard balls' fell, while overnight frosts froze the water in the billycans and particularly affected the camels. The men could keep reasonably warm around campfires whilst they drank tea and smoked their pipes, but it rained so much that their clothes never had a chance to dry out properly. The canvas tents were soaked through and the wet equipment became very heavy to lift. As the roads deteriorated, the wagons ground to a halt and the camels slithered through the bogs. They were ill-adapted for the terrain, as the pads on their feet had evolved for deserts, not the swamp-like surfaces of Australia. In the worst-affected places the wagon wheels disappeared and the drivers had to wade into the boggy area, dig the axles free and lay branches in the wheel ruts to provide enough traction for them to get out again. All this resulted in delays on the first part of the journey which had not been allowed for during the planning stages.

On their third day, one of the sepoys resigned. As a Hindu, he was not permitted to eat the salt beef which the rest of the party feasted on, and his diet had been confined to bread and water. Now he was starving, and he asked Landells to release him from the expedition.

As the others continued northwards, the wagons broke down every day. It was apparent that they had taken too much in the way of supplies, with inadequate transport. Captain Francis Cadell of the Royal Society had offered to transport the supplies to Adelaide by ship and then up the Murray and Darling rivers as far as Menindee, to be collected en route. This would have eliminated the need for the wagons which regularly broke down, and saved the horses and camels for the more arduous roads further north. Burke had rejected the plan, as he thought that transporting the supplies via Adelaide would give the South Australians a chance to interfere and delay the expedition. Moreover, Captain Cadell had strongly opposed Burke's appointment as leader of the expedition and instead favoured another candidate, Peter Egerton Warburton, a police officer who had previously undertaken some expeditions across Australia. Agreeing that this would be a far more efficient way of transporting the supplies, Dr Beckler had urged Burke to accept the offer, but the latter was too proud and too cautious to entrust the supplies to someone whom he regarded as a rival at best, an enemy – and a defeated one at that – at worst, and refused to discuss it.

Each morning they woke at dawn to the sound of the Chinese gong, got up and stoked the campfire. After making tea they had breakfast: hunks of damper, a traditional Australian wheat and flour-based soda bread, baked over a campfire and filled with salt beef. Sometimes the camels were tethered or kept in night paddocks, and at other times they were let loose, but as a rule they never walked further than a few miles, so little time was spent or wasted in rounding them up for the next day. The rain, however, made the harnesses slippery and stiff, and the buckles were difficult to tighten. It therefore took between two and three hours to organise the packs and hoist them onto the horses and camels using a pulley system slung over the branch of a tree.

The main party usually set off at about half-past nine each morning, with Burke and the horses going ahead, followed by Landells and the camels, Wills next, and the wagons behind. They travelled for about twelve hours per day, stopping briefly for lunch and occasionally a smoking break. Although generally exhausted by the time they reached camp, they still had two hours of further work: feeding and watering the animals, unloading supplies and mending broken equipment. At night the tents were pitched, the campfire was lit, stew was made and loaves of fresh damper were cooked in the camp ovens. While the men sat smoking and talking around the campfire, Wills and the scientists retired to their tents to write up their journals.

The conscientious young student remained true to form throughout his life, carefully keeping his diary every day, especially during the early stages of the expedition. His initial chronicles included a set of scientific records consisting of up to fifteen daily meteorological readings, followed by pages of navigational calculations. The most useful tool in Wills' armoury was a prismatic compass, with which he set their course and kept to it as far as possible, depending on the roughness of the terrain. When they were faced with the obstacles of rocky outcrops, rivers and boggy country, slight recalculations were called for. Some patches of open desert completely lacked reference points, and the expedition members kept as far as possible to their predetermined bearing for several days on end, with no definite aim. He had to calculate the distance travelled each day in order to compile a map, which he did generally from guessing speed over a fixed distance.

Latitude, their north-south position, was established by measuring the sun's altitude with a sextant and an artificial horizon: a pool of mercury enclosed in a vibration-proof box. Wills looked through a system of lenses until he saw dual suns reflected in a mirror, then moved an index arm on the sextant until the two suns were superimposed and read off an angle from the scale of the instrument. Several pairs of readings were needed for an accurate calculation. In windy weather, he found that it was rarely possible to keep the mirror free from dust even for a few seconds, and this interfered with the readings of the spirit level, so that altitudes taken with the horizon were not particularly accurate. Once he had obtained satisfactory altitude readings, or sometimes the best he could given the circumstances, Wills used a special set of tables from a nautical almanac to calculate latitude. Longitude was established by comparing local time with that at a fixed point such as the Greenwich meridian. As the earth was known to revolve fifteen degrees every hour, if one knew the difference between the two times, he could calculate longitude. To find out the local time, Wills used his sextant to determine when the sun reached its highest point, this being dependent on the accuracy of his chronometers. Over a desert expedition, variations of several degrees were to be expected. Moreover, such instruments had to be used with extreme care. The earlier explorers Charles Sturt and John McDouall Stuart had both damaged their eyesight by taking sun sightings in the Australian desert. Wills avoided doing likewise; he was skilled at taking star sightings, and preferred to do so in the evening. When the night sky was clear he spent about one and a half hours, perhaps more, working out the altitude and position of particular stars. Then, using his astronomical tables, he could calculate his latitude and longitude without having to 'shoot the sun'.

Unlike Wills, Burke kept only a very basic diary, and then only sporadically, comprising less than 1,000 words in total, although he may have written more which did not survive. His brief entries were contained in a leather-bound pocket book, smudged with red earth. He had been asked by the Exploration Committee to keep a detailed record of the journey, but he was too impatient to do so. Although he sometimes read Wills' journal and made a few suggestions, it appears that Burke's efforts to do any more were half-hearted at best. While employed in the police force at Melbourne, he had always been reluctant to attend to his paperwork; he lacked the discipline to do so, and was not about to break the habits of a lifetime.

By the end of the first week, the expedition had only covered about 60 miles, and the wagons were still some way behind the expedition members. They were encamped at the hamlet of Mia Mia when Burke allowed them a day of rest on Sunday, 26 August. It was not, however, a day off for the artist Ludwig Becker, who was ordered by Burke to sort out the accounts and expenditure that they had incurred so far. Spectators from Mia Mia were fascinated by the arrival of the party, of whom they had read so much in the local newspapers, and they could not resist the opportunity to come and look.

As devoted a son as ever, Wills took this opportunity to write to his father, assuring him that they were:

> all right enough, except as regards cleanliness, and everything has gone well, barring the necessary break-downs, and wet weather. We have to travel slowly, on account of the camels. I suppose Professor Neumayer will overtake us in a day or two. I have been agreeably disappointed in my idea of the camels. They are far from unpleasant to ride; in fact, it is much less fatiguing than riding on horseback, and even with the little practice I have yet had, I find it shakes me less.

Within a few days, Wills had happily adapted further to riding on the camels. On 31 August he wrote to Mr Byerly that it was:

> a much more pleasant process than I anticipated, and for my work I find it much better than riding on horseback. The saddles, as you are aware, are double, so I sit on the back portion behind the hump, and pack my instruments in front, I can thus ride on, keeping my journal and making calculations; and need only stop the camel when I want to take any bearings carefully; but the barometers can be read and registered without halting. The animals are very quiet, and easily managed, much more so than horses.

By this time, some members of the expedition had realised that they were expected to undertake duties they had not envisioned beforehand. In particular, the artist and naturalist Ludwig Becker, who at 53 was the oldest of the team, imagined that he would be doing little more than the tasks of painting and recording the expedition for posterity. It came as a rude surprise when he found he was expected to look after the accounts for Burke, as well as help load boxes and lead camels like an ordinary stable lad. It was significant of the generally confused motives of the committee and expedition that most of the Royal Society thought and hoped that the expedition would undertake a thorough scientific examination of the continent. Few were yet aware that Burke was something of a loose cannon; an adventurer with ill-defined, not to say fatalistic, notions of romanticism and the thrill of being an adventurer, who regarded the scientists as an encumbrance and would probably have been much happier had they stayed behind.

In reality Wills was the one scientist who proved himself indispensable. Though only third-in-command, he was arguably the driving force on the expedition. To him fell the duty of taking samples and of keeping detailed records of the distance travelled daily, of the lay of the land, watercourses, water quality, soil types, geological formations and of the occurrence of minerals or gems. He was to sketch specimens, like Becker, but in addition Wills' duties included the drawing of maps on a regular basis; measuring compass variations; recording meteorological conditions including rainfall, temperature, wind speeds, whirlwinds, thunderstorms, dust storms and similar occurrences; to say nothing of astronomical observations including the paths of meteors and patterns of stars. As well as these tasks, he was responsible for navigating the party across the continent, and lastly, he was the only one of them who could use a compass and sextant.

Such a venture was bound to test personal relationships, and irreconcilable differences between the leaders were not long in coming to the surface. Burke had always been at least mildly resentful of the fact that the committee had given Landells special responsibility for the camels. As long as the animals gave no trouble, he was prepared to accept them, if somewhat grudgingly. Nevertheless, he preferred to ride on ahead of everyone else on his horse, leaving Landells, Wills, Becker and Dr Beckler to travel on foot with the animals. As he became increasingly uncommunicative with the men, morale began to suffer. Wills, who had always kept very much to himself, was probably bothered least of all. To him the success of the expedition was the most important thing, and personal relations probably did not enter into it as long as they did not fall out and could work together. Yet the others were increasingly resentful, especially when Burke took to passing his time in inns en route during the evening, instead of associating with and talking problems through with them.

Wills continued, conscientiously, to immerse himself in his usual tasks, while Landells and Ferguson had to deal with the recurring problems of loose horses, stray camels and perpetually overloaded wagons – which with their continual breaking down severely tested everyone's patience. Landells felt that Burke was being too impatient in wanting to forge on regardless. He believed that the camels had been given insufficient time to graze on what little pasture there was available, and that the severe weather was taking its toll on animals that were acclimatised to tropical conditions. Dr Beckler seconded him, as he too noticed the animals were beginning to suffer from the effects of continual rain, the gradual change of feed and camping in the open. They developed various ailments, including catarrh and diarrhoea, and gave evidence of other digestion problems. Added to this was the attitude of the Melbourne press, which was starting as a whole to take Burke to task for his inexperience. One paper remarked that Landells was 'the most capable man of the party', and the only one who appeared to be completely at ease, whereas the correspondent could find almost nothing to say about Burke, except that he had 'the air of a leader about him', and had 'a large well-shaped head'.

Later that week, as the expedition reached the outskirts of Bendigo, about 90 miles north-west of Melbourne, a party was held by the town's dignitaries for the explorers. Burke took the chance to defend himself against the expectations of those who wanted results with astonishing speed, asking everyone to be patient and allow them 'full and fair trial'. Wills and Landells left at ten o'clock that evening, though some of the other men stayed on later, drinking well rather than wisely and inevitably starting later than usual the following morning.

When they reached the small village of Swan Hill on 6 September, some 200 miles from Melbourne on the River Murray, most of the residents turned out to greet them as they rode past the houses. Here they were to leave their hired wagons. However, Burke was worried when he received a telegram threatening him with imprisonment for a dishonoured cheque for £96, something which could have endangered his standing with the Royal Society, and he had to contact a friend asking him to stand security for the debt. The expedition was proving more costly than anticipated, with the wagons proving increasingly slow and costing £83 in repairs in the first week alone. The drivers had not anticipated how hard the going would be, and demanded more pay.

Wills was expecting to welcome an old friend at Swan Hill, as Professor Neumayer from the observatory was due to temporarily join the expedition. He intended to travel with the party towards Menindee, by the River

Darling, to try and further his research into the earth's magnetism. From Swan Hill on 8 September Wills wrote to his father, reporting on their progress so far:

> We are all in good health and spirits. The road we are about to take is not that which I had anticipated, namely, down the side of the Lower Darling, as we hear there is literally nothing for the horses to eat; so that we are going right across the country to the Darling, passing the Murray at this place. We leave Swan Hill about the middle of next week, and shall then be out of the colony of Victoria. We are expecting Professor Neumayer up shortly, – a scrap of paper to-day by the postman says to-morrow. I am rather disappointed at not having yet an assistant surveyor, but I hope he will arrive shortly. Letters in future had better be directed to the care of Dr Macadam, the secretary, as they will have to go by sea.

They spent five days at Swan Hill before moving on. As they went, Burke discharged another of the sepoys, who had become too ill to work. Three other men were discharged at the same time, and four new men taken on. The foreman, Charles Ferguson, was becoming increasingly unpopular and began to complain about his pay. Burke threatened to reduce his salary, but Ferguson responded by threatening to leave, and Burke was forced to back down in order to keep him.

As they approached Balranald, New South Wales, their journey was hampered by more bad weather and the roads were becoming very narrow. The wagon drivers insisted that their loads be reduced or the horses would collapse. Having hauled the supplies for about three weeks at considerable expense, Burke decided the only thing to do was to hold an auction of equipment in the village, including some of the ammunition and sets of blacksmiths' tools. They also left behind some of the lime juice, which had been brought to help prevent scurvy.

Burke also decided to discharge six more men. He told Ludwig Becker, foreman Charles Ferguson and Brahe, Langan, James McIlwaine and Belooch to stay behind at Balranald, promising he would send for them a little later. Despite his military training, he generally shrank from confrontation or giving people bad news. Perhaps Ferguson saw through the ploy, for he challenged Burke to a bare-knuckle fight and had to be physically restrained by the others. Taken by surprise, Burke said at first that he wanted him to stay, but later thought better of it and took him aside, saying that he had to admit the truth. He then offered to retain Ferguson and Langan at reduced salaries, but they refused. Burke issued their wage cheques as normal – probably aware that local bank staff and shopkeepers knew the expedition was financially strained and would be unlikely to honour them. A little later, Becker, Brahe and Belooch rejoined the main party, but Ferguson, Langan and McIlwaine were left behind.

When the expedition had left Melbourne the previous month, Dr Wills had remarked to one of the committee members on Charles Ferguson's appearance and general demeanour. When Ferguson returned to Melbourne, the foreman published his own account of the affair, and took the Exploration Committee to court, winning an undisclosed sum for unfair dismissal. By then, those who might have disproved his statements were dead.

From Balranald on 17 September Wills wrote to his mother. He told her that they were at the last major township before they made their way towards the interior:

> It is an out-of-the-way place, situated on the lower part of the Murrumbidgee River. Our journey so far has been very satisfactory: we are most fortunate as regards the season, for there has been more rain this winter than has been known for the last four or five years. In fact, it seems probable that we shall finish our work in a much shorter period than was anticipated; very likely in ten or twelve months. The country up here is beautiful; everything green and pleasant; and if you saw it now, you would not believe that in two months' time it could have such a parched and barren appearance as it will then assume.

Despite Wills' continued optimism, they were not a happy band. Burke's style of leadership continued to cause discontent among the others, most of whom complained that he did not choose camping places until after dark, sometimes after midnight, and they could thus not check beforehand whether there would be suitable grazing pasture for the camels. Whenever they moved on to a new camp, too many axes, spades and other tools were left behind as Burke was so careless in tidying up or delegating anyone else to do so. Burke himself was becoming increasingly impatient, especially at the slow speed of the wagons, and on their way to Menindee he decided he would travel ahead of the main expedition party and leave Dr Beckler to supervise the wagons.

Another of Burke's bad decisions was to take what he thought would be a shortcut across country, instead of following a recognised track from Balranald to Menindee on the River Darling. This took them across difficult soft terrain, where the wagon wheels sunk deep into the sandy soil and had to be regularly dug out with a shovel. The horses did not fare much better, and were so tired that they had to stop and rest at frequent intervals. When the animals could go no further, they were unhitched from the wagons and taken to a waterhole for refreshment. The wagons were left temporarily abandoned, while Burke and Wills rode on ahead. Cheerfully oblivious at first, the forward party later lost valuable time having to go back and rescue them.

Wills spent much of his time immersed in his surveying work, and it is fair to assume that he was concentrating so much on this and on his diary that he had little idea of the internal politics and problems between the others. Had he been aware of these, one wonders whether he would have risen to the occasion and tried to exert some influence as a peacemaker himself. He may have realised that the obstinate Burke would have been unlikely to accept such advice, and being a serious-minded man, doubtless assumed that there were more important things to be done than to get involved in petty jealousies between individuals unless it was unavoidable.

Professor Neumayer had always intended his presence on the expedition to be temporary, only as long as it took him to collect his 'magnetic data', and by the end of September he was preparing to return to Melbourne. Wills had enjoyed his company, and despite his impatience with scientists generally, Burke had got on well with him too. On Neumayer's last evening with them, all three discussed the possibility of a relief vessel being sent to the north coast to meet the expedition, and it was agreed that Burke would give this further thought and write to the Exploration Committee from Menindee if he thought this was necessary.

The departure of Neumayer released Burke from some of his unwelcome obligations. The latter was aware that there was now no likelihood of reports being sent back to the Royal Society, and on 1 October he confronted the scientists in the party. He told them that from now on, they were going to have to walk all the way up to the Gulf of Carpentaria in order to lessen the burden on the horses and camels, which would be required to carry the stores. He informed a dismayed Becker and Dr Beckler that they would now have to give up their naturalist and botanic investigations, respectively, and work like the rest of the men, doing any tasks which might be required of them. At the same time, they would have to limit their materials and anything else required for their investigations. From now on, they would be allowed just 30lb of personal equipment each. For the scientists, this would mean leaving behind nearly all their instruments. They were furious, yet had no option but to agree.

Burke then told Landells that the wagons were carrying too much weight, and the camels would have to carry an extra 400lb. In heavy rain and thunderstorms, the stores had to be completely reorganised and Becker, on whom the responsibility for this fell, found it extremely arduous. He had worked very hard during the daytime and had had no sleep for the last two nights, but spared himself nothing as he did his share of getting up at five o'clock to help saddle and load the camels, lifting heavy canvas bags of flower and sugar to be fastened and put on the pack-saddle, his fingernails becoming split and bent in the process.

Landells was angry that the camels were being overloaded before the expedition reached the edge of the desert. He was genuinely concerned for their welfare, and also saw this as counter to the authority which he had been given. Landells considered he was their keeper, completely in charge of the camels, making sure they were not overburdened and ensuring they were given plenty of water. Burke was impatient with them because they often ran away and had to be rounded up, they were slower than the horses and they took longer to load.

It did not escape the notice of Becker and Dr Beckler that Wills was increasingly being left in charge of certain aspects of the expedition. Burke was becoming lazy and progressively more disinclined to bother with detail. He also disliked confrontation, and perhaps there was a measure of cowardice involved. The less mercurial, more conscientious Wills could be relied on to do some of his chief's dirty work if necessary. Burke should have been leaning more on Landells as his deputy, but with both men becoming ever more estranged he chose not to do so.

On 2 October they reached Bilbarka on the River Darling. Burke learned that a steamer, owned by one Captain Johnston, was heading north along the coast to Menindee. Thankfully, the steamer had no connections with his old opponent at the Royal Society, Captain Francis Cadell. In light of this, Burke thought that this would solve the problem of doing away with the wagons, which he found were proving a burden. It was only gradually dawning on him that the supplies they were taking with them were seriously impeding their progress. He therefore asked his men to reorganise the stores so that they could free themselves of 8 tonnes of equipment, which could be loaded onto the steamer and sent north to Menindee where they would be unloaded at a suitable depot. Increasingly impatient with what he regarded as 'useless baggage', he would not be unduly concerned if he never saw any of this again. While this was being done, he continued to argue with Landells. There was a disagreement over 60 gallons of rum that Landells had brought to feed to the camels in the belief that it would prevent them from getting scurvy and would toughen up their feet, better preparing the animals for rough terrain – it was commonly thought that urine with a high alcohol content stiffened leather. There was also a theory that the crafty Landells may merely have brought the rum to sell on the black market during the journey at a handsome profit – and nobody need be any the wiser. Whatever the case, the argument was no doubt exacerbated because Landells was increasingly dissatisfied with Burke, and regarded him as a madman who would lead them into danger and be the death of them yet.

It was not long before all their arguments came to a head. Landells probably resented not having been appointed leader of the expedition; he considered himself superior in intellect to Burke, as well as temperamentally more able to lead. There were suspicions that Landells had been trying to sow dissension among the others, particularly with Becker, Dr Beckler and Wills. The two former were plainly exasperated with Burke, but Wills was thus far too loyal to get involved. On 4 October Landells and Wills went together to post some letters in Bilbarka. As they walked, Landells made several very critical remarks about Burke which Wills thought were quite uncalled for. One of them was that Burke had 'no right to interfere about the camels', after he had privately made agreements with the committee, of which Burke had no knowledge. Landells told Wills that everything was being mismanaged, and that if their leader had his way, 'everything would go to the devil'.

Wills was unimpressed by Landells, and may have had his doubts about how long the latter would stay in the expedition. In a letter to his friend Richard Birnie, he had praised Burke as 'an energetic, good-natured, rough, gentlemanly fellow'. His opinion of Landells was less favourable, and while he admitted that he was excellent in managing the camels, he was 'nothing of a gentleman, either in manners or feeling'. He may have been sentimental and good-natured, particularly where animals were concerned, but he was not good with his colleagues – 'he must always make people dislike him, from his unmannerly diffidence and want of substance'.[2]

71

The last straw came on 7 October when a group of shearers from a nearby sheep station broke into the expedition's store and made free with the alcoholic refreshment available. Some members of the expedition had probably been helping themselves to rum, though they had taken care not to drink themselves into a stupor. However, the shearers were less careful, and stories of drunkenness soon found their way into the local press. When Burke heard he was furious, and ordered Landells to leave the rum behind. Landells told Burke angrily that if this happened, he would not be responsible for the animals' welfare. Burke said he could do as he pleased, and then walked out. Once he was gone, Landells called Wills to take delivery of his papers from the government, saying he intended to leave for Melbourne at once. After promising to hand over the camels, some of which had wandered off in pursuit of suitable grazing, as they did regularly at camp, he went and told the wagon drivers that he was leaving. The news spread all over the astonished camp in very little time.

While everyone was getting ready to move on, Wills thought that he ought to make sure Burke was aware of what was happening. As if to imply that he thought Landells nothing better than a prima donna who would soon come to his senses, Burke said he would take no notice of such 'news' until it was brought to him officially. When Landells came back, he asked Burke to dismiss him immediately, in the presence of Wills. Burke refused, saying he would forward his resignation if he wished it, with a recommendation that he should be paid up to that time. Landells was not satisfied with this; he wanted to portray himself in the eyes of the public as the injured party, ill-treated by an arrogant and incapable leader. Nevertheless, he had repeatedly told Wills that he did not intend to stay with the expedition long. He confided in the surveyor that he was sure Burke was a rash madman, that he had no idea what he was doing, that he would 'make a mess of the whole thing' and ruin them all, and that he did not consider himself safe in the same tent as Burke. While he made some of these remarks in the presence of Becker and Dr Beckler, he reserved his most serious allegations for the ears of Wills alone.

On 8 October Landells spoke to William Hodgkinson, an experienced bushman and until recently a journalist with the *Melbourne Weekly Age*, who had joined the expedition at Swan Hill. He asked Hodgkinson to help him draft a letter of resignation, and then said that if Burke would allow him unqualified charge of the camels, he would be prepared to reconsider. For a couple of days, it looked as if he would change his mind, but on reflection Landells realised that he could no longer work under Burke.

The scandal made for many a lively story in the Melbourne press. Landells had returned to the city, eager to justify his actions, but soon found that most of the press were on Burke's side. A letter from Landells putting his views forward was printed and speedily followed by a rejoinder from Wills, who accused the former second-in-command of 'playing a fine game trying to set us all together by the ears'. He quoted Burke as saying that Landells had been abusing and finding fault with them all, that Landells positively 'hated' Wills, who had previously believed they were the best of friends, and that Landells had been speaking ill to him of Burke, Becker and Dr Beckler, to the point where it was as if there was virtually no man in the party who had not urged Burke to dismiss Landells. Wills' letter was criticised by some sections of the Melbourne press as 'dictated by evident dislike of Mr Landells', and some thought he had been intriguing against Landells in order to obtain the post of second-in-command. Others thought that both men were as bad as each other, 'utterly incapable of appreciating the magnificent opportunity of distinction' which their appointments to the expedition had conferred on them.[3]

Dr Beckler attempted to resign at the same time, saying he did not like the manner in which Burke had spoken to Landells. Embarrassed by what they saw as unseemly quarrels between grown men who ought to know better, the Exploration Committee accepted their resignations, taking the opportunity to reaffirm their confidence in Burke's leadership. Their opinion was by no means unanimous. The treasurer, Dr David Wilkie, declared at a meeting on 10 November in the presence of journalists that Burke should never have been appointed; Landells was known to be unfit for his position; and Wills 'was nothing more than a child, a protégé of Professor Neumayer, who had given him a few lessons in astronomy and surveying, and sent him out with the expedition to complete his education'.[4] At a private meeting William Nicholson, the chief secretary, had also been critical of Wills, although less scathing, commenting that while he liked what he had seen of the surveyor, he had not yet proved his capacity for command and was still very inexperienced.

Public opinion, like that of the press, was largely on the side of Burke. Melbourne's leading newspaper, the *Melbourne Argus*, noted that Landells had 'deserted his leader on the eve of the fight; and such an act, so subversive of all discipline, renders all explanations contemptible'. Unamused by the washing of such dirty linen in public, the *Melbourne Herald* begged to differ, saying that 'petty details of the small personal bickering and tattling that went on in the camp are utterly unworthy of serious record', and Wills 'ought not to have condescended upon journalising them'. This obsession with 'such contemptible trifles' demonstrated merely that 'the spirit of elevated enthusiasm' with which the expedition had set out had well and truly evaporated. That the mild-mannered Wills should have expressed himself so forcefully might be taken as a measure of his indignation; alternatively, it may have merely been the dutiful defence by a loyal lieutenant of the leader whom he had pledged to stand by through thick and thin.

Wills was now promoted to second-in-command. He was less headstrong and impulsive, more loyal than Landells, and there was no danger of any rivalry between the men or further in-fighting. It was as if those on the expedition were falling into two groups, the younger men like Wills, who were genuinely inspired by Burke's enthusiasm and were prepared to overlook his faults, and the older men like Landells, who resented the slapdash, impulsive former police officer who treated them like cadets or schoolboys. There may also have been an element of xenophobia on the part of Landells and others, who regarded themselves as superior to the Irish; racial prejudice against the Irish being rife among some sections of society at the time.

Unhappily, Burke now made another error in choosing William Wright as third-in-command. The sudden loss of Landells and imminent departure of Dr Beckler had left him with little alternative but to settle the issue as speedily as possible. Wright had until recently been manager of a sheep station, but the business was being sold and he was looking for alternative employment. Burke had met him by chance in a bar when they arrived in Menindee at the end of October, and he found out that Wright had recently returned from a journey towards Cooper's Creek and was keen to undertake further exploration. When Wright volunteered to act as a guide on the expedition, Burke agreed to take him on, despite having neither knowledge nor experience of Wright's abilities. The latter would soon prove a poor judge of situations and ungrateful for the trust placed in him. When he eventually lost any respect he might have had for Burke, Wright told others that the Irishman was 'gone to destruction and would lose all who were with him'. Yet Burke had thought Wright would be the man in effect to take the place, although not the same position in the hierarchy, of Landells and Dr Beckler.

Without Landells there was a new beginning. It might have augured well for the expedition that Burke and Wills were equally dedicated to its success, and that between them there was mutual loyalty and respect. Burke told John King that he loved Wills 'as a brother', and to others praised him as 'a capital officer, zealous and untiring'. Wills repaid the compliment, mentioning in one of his letters to his father that 'the more I see of Mr Burke the more I like him'. The surveyor and new second-in-command was never anything less than a loyal lieutenant, always prepared to accept his leader's authority. If he ever had any doubts about Burke's abilities and judgement – and there were surely times when he did – he was too faithful to say so. As history would later prove, it might have been better for all concerned if he had occasionally spoken out and made an alternative, often more sensible, view known.

5

From Cooper's Creek to Carpentaria

After travelling about 460 miles since leaving Melbourne at the end of August, a journey the regular mail coach generally completed in just over a week, the expedition party reached Menindee on 14 October. By this time two of the five officers had resigned, thirteen members had been dismissed, and eight new men had been hired. Wills was aware that Burke considered them to be, in effect, rivals of John McDouall Stuart, who had accepted a challenge from the South Australian government a year previously. If Stuart made the first successful south–north crossing of the continent west of the 143rd line of longitude, his reward would be £2,000. Burke's impatience was partly borne of his concern that Stuart might beat him to the north coast, and he was increasingly irritated with their slow progress which often averaged only 2 miles an hour. Wills felt powerless to try to influence his determined, stubborn leader.

In Menindee Burke decided to split the group. Taking the strong-est horses, seven of the fittest men and a small amount of equipment he intended to push on quickly to Cooper's Creek, which the committee had chosen as the centre of the expedition's operations, and then wait for the supplies and the others to catch up. This first group left Menindee on 19 October, guided by William Wright. They left behind a second group which included Ludwig Becker and Dr Hermann Beckler, who had reluctantly agreed to stay on for the time being despite Becker having been fired once and Beckler attempting to resign.

Travel was relatively easy for Burke's reduced party; recent heavy rain had ensured a plentiful supply of water and they found creeks at regular distances of 20 miles or less, while unusually mild weather saw temperatures exceed 90°F (32.2°C) only twice before reaching Cooper's Creek. At the midpoint of Torowoto Swamp, Wright was sent back to Menindee alone to bring up the remainder of the men and supplies, and Burke continued on to Cooper's Creek.

Whilst at Torowoto Swamp, on 29 October, Burke and Wills wrote and forwarded a despatch to the committee, including a brief report from the former and a detailed surveying report from the latter. These documents confirmed that both leaders, and a party consisting of Wright, Brahe, Patton, McDonough, King, Gray, Dost Mahomet, fifteen horses and sixteen camels, had all left Menindee ten days earlier. Wright had volunteered to show them a practical route towards Cooper's Creek, a distance of about 100 miles from the River Darling. This stage of the journey had gone more smoothly than they had expected, as they had travelled mainly through fine sheep-grazing country, ideal for the horses and camels, at a speed of 20 miles a day.

Burke was optimistic about the terrain, saying that 'the country improves as we go on'. The previous day, between Wanominta and Paldrumata Creek, they had travelled:

> over a splendid grazing country, and to-day, we are encamped on a creek or swamp, the banks of which are very well grassed, and good feed all the way from our last camp, except for two miles, where the ground was barren and swampy. Of course it is impossible for me to say what effect an unusually dry summer would produce throughout this country, or whether we are now travelling in an unusually favourable season or not. I describe things as I find them.

Burke also confirmed that Wright had been made third-in-command, subject to the committee's approval, from the day of their departure from Menindee, and he hoped that they would agree to the appointment. If Wright was allowed to take the instructions that Burke had given him, he was sure they would work well together, 'and if the committee think proper to make inquiries with regard to him they will find that he is well qualified for the post, and that he bears the very highest character'. At that time,

Burke's plans were to leave a depot at Cooper's Creek, and then to proceed beyond that point with a small party. He reconsidered dividing the party again, however, after Wright had warned him that they might meet with opposition from the aborigines.

In his new second-in-command, Burke had every confidence, and he could not have chosen better. Wills, he wrote, was 'a capital officer, zealous and untiring in the performance of his duties, and I trust that he will remain my second as long as I am in charge of the expedition'. The other men, he added, 'all conduct themselves admirably, and they are all most anxious to go on; but the committee may rely upon it that I shall go on steadily and carefully, and that I shall endeavour not to lose a chance or to run any unnecessary risk'.

In his surveyor's report, Wills remarked on the countryside close to the eastern bank of the River Darling as presenting 'the most barren and miserable appearance of any land' they had yet come across, consisting mostly of mud flats, covered with polygonum bushes, box timber and a few plants of inferior quality. Further on the land improved into fair grazing country. However, the constant shortage of water made it unsuitable for occupation, and would probably continue to do so for some years. Sand ridges 20–40ft high, sometimes even more than 60ft above the level of the river banks, would form almost insuperable barriers in the way of anyone trying to conduct water from the river by means of canals. Wills was sure that the difficulties with which settlers had to contend arose not so much from the absorbent nature of the soil, as from the want of anything to absorb. The last season was said to have been the wettest for several years, yet everything looked so parched he would have assumed it had been an unusually dry one. At least they had been fortunate with the weather, in being able to travel in moderate temperatures.

Burke and Wills – accompanied by their reduced forward party consisting of Brahe, King, Gray, Patton, McDonough, Dost Mahomet, fifteen horses and sixteen camels – reached Cooper's Creek on 11 November. In 1860 this was the edge of the area previously explored by Europeans, the river having been visited by Captain Charles Sturt in 1845 and Augustus Charles Gregory in 1858. On arrival, the party formed a depot at the creek while they conducted reconnaissance to the north. A plague of rats forced the men to move camp, however, and they formed a second depot further downstream at Bullah Bullah waterhole, where they erected a stockade and named the place Fort Wills.

Five days later, Wills went out on a series of short journeys on his own to explore the surrounding desert area. His reasons were twofold. Firstly, he wanted to plan what he thought would be the best route – the shortest practicable cut – towards the Gulf of Carpentaria, preferably by a northern or north-eastward direction. Secondly, their water supplies were rapidly running out and he was anxious to find more. What he found were large tracts of sandhill country, with small salt lakes, partly surrounded by small trees and shrubs. Disappointed at failing in his aim, he returned to camp. On his next reconnaissance Wills sought extra help and took McDonough with him. They set out with three camels, walked about 80 miles in two days, and searched for water until they were exhausted. Believing the camels were probably equally tired, they set the beasts loose whilst McDonough prepared supper. To their horror, they realised a short time later that the apparently exhausted camels were rejuvenated and ambling off into the distance. As Wills noted ruefully, they were 'not nearly so done up as they appeared to be'.[1] Stranded in the heat without their pack animals and only a small supply of water, rapidly going off and in a leaking bag, they had no alternative but to return, redoubling their search for any pools.

On 6 December Wills wrote to his sister from Cooper's Creek. It was so hot he found it impracticable to use quick-drying ink, and he apologised for writing with a pencil. He told Bessy that they had been there for three weeks and hoped to continue north in about a fortnight, he also described to her their recent venture:

Everything has been very comfortable so far; in fact, more like a picnic party than a serious exploration: but I suppose we shall have some little difficulties to contend with soon. I had an intimation of something of the kind a few days ago, having been out reconnoitring the country to the north for three days, with one man and three camels, and had found no water, so that the animals were very thirsty, and on the third night managed to get away from us, leaving us about eighty miles from the main camp, without hay or water, except what remained of that which we had brought with us; so there was nothing for it, but to walk home as soon as we could, carrying as much water as possible, to be drunk on the way. After searching about in order to be sure that the camels had gone home, we started at about half-past seven, and were lucky enough to find a creek with some water in it about ten miles on, where we remained until evening; for it is dry work travelling in the middle of the day, with the thermometer varying from 90 to 105 degrees in the shade, and about 140 degrees in the sun ...

By the end of their journey, Wills and McDonough had less than half a pint of water left between them:

When we stopped to rest the second night, it had been blowing a hot wind all day, with the thermometer at 107 degrees in the shade. This made us require more water than usual. I can assure you there is nothing like a walk of this sort to make one appreciate the value of a drink of cold water. We feel no inclination for anything else, and smack our lips over a drop such as you would not think of tasting, with as much relish as ever any one did over the best sherry or champagne ... I hope by the time that this reaches you we shall not only have been entirely across, but back here again, and possibly on our way to Melbourne. There is no probability of the expedition lasting two or three years. I expect to be in town again within twelve months from the time of starting ... To give you an idea of Cooper's Creek, fancy extensive flat, sandy plains, covered with herbs dried like hay, and imagine a creek or river, somewhat similar in appearance and size to the Dart above the Weir, winding its way through these flats, having its banks densely clothed with gum trees and other evergreens: – so far there appears to be a considerable resemblance, but now for the difference. The water of Cooper's Creek is the colour of flood-water in the Dart; the latter is a continuous running stream; Cooper's Creek is only a number of waterholes. In some places it entirely disappears, the water in flood-time spreading all over the flats and forming no regular channel. The flies are very numerous, so that one can do nothing without having a veil on; and whilst eating the only plan is to wear goggles.

In his report from Cooper's Creek of 13 December, Burke also referred to the loss of the animals:

... and he and the man who accompanied him were obliged to return on foot, which they accomplished in forty-eight hours. Fortunately, upon their return they found a pool of water. The three camels have not yet been recovered. Mr Wills co-operates cordially with me. He is a most zealous and efficient officer.

The missing camels proved able to look after themselves, and several months later they were found near Adelaide.

On 15 December Wills produced a lengthy report, over 5,000 words long, which he had compiled whilst they waited at Cooper's Creek for Wright and their supplies to catch up. In addition to giving precise details of the latitude and longitude of the journey they had taken, he made detailed observations on the terrain. North of Torowoto Swamp, he noted that the country was not so well grassed or watered as that to the south, and much of it was subject to flooding. 'Nearly all the water met with was thick and muddy: it was met with in small clay pans, most of which would probably be dry in three weeks.' He also wrote at length on the vegetation, wildlife, temperatures of land and water, and the directions of the wind. Two short passages will testify to his industry, one on Cooper's Creek itself and the other on his 'meteorological remarks':

At the point at which we first struck Cooper's Creek it was rocky, sandy, and dry; but about half a mile further down we came to some good waterholes, where the bed of the creek was very boggy, and the banks richly grassed with kangaroo and other grasses. The general course is a little north of west, but it winds about very much between high sand hills. The waterholes are not large, but deep, and well shaded, both by the steep banks and the numerous box trees surrounding them. The logs and bushes high upon the forks of the trees, tell of the destructive floods to which this part of the country has been sub-jected, and that at no very distant period, as may be seen by the flood marks on trees of not more than five or six years' growth.

It would be rather premature for me to offer any opinion on the climate of Cooper's Creek on so short a stay, and my other duties have prevented me from making any observations that would be worth forwarding in detail ... neither on the creek, nor during the journey up, have we experienced any extreme temperatures: the heat, although considerably greater here than in Melbourne, as shown by a thermometer, is not felt more severely by us. The maximum daily temperatures since our arrival on Cooper's Creek have generally exceeded 100 degrees [farenheit]; the highest of all was registered on November 27th ... when the thermometer stood at 109 degrees in the shade. There was at that time a strong wind from the north, which felt rather warm, but had not the peculiar characteristics of a hot wind. One of the most noticeable features in the weather has been the well-marked regular-ity in the course of the wind, which almost invariably blew lightly from the east or south-east soon after sunrise, went gradually round to north by two o'clock, sometimes blowing fresh from that quarter, followed the sun to west by sunset, and then died away or blew gently from the south throughout the night. A sudden change took place yesterday, December 14th; the day had been unusually hot, temperature of air at one p.m. 106°, at which time cirrocumulus clouds began to cross the sky from north-west, and at two p.m. the wind sprang up in the south-west, blowing with great violence (force 6); it soon shifted to south, increasing in force to (7) and sometimes (8); it continued to blow from the same quarter all night, and has not yet much abated. Once during the night it lulled for about an hour, and then commenced again; it is now (four p.m.) blowing with a force of (5) from south by east, with a clear sky. Before the wind had sprung up the sky had become overcast, and we were threatened with a thunderstorm; rain was evidently falling in the west and north-west, but the sky partially cleared in the evening without our receiving any. Flashes of distant lightning were visible towards the north. During the night, the thunderstorm from the north approached sufficiently near for thunder to be distinctly heard; the flashes of lightning were painfully brilliant, although so far away. The storm passed to the south-east without reaching us; the sky remained overcast until between eight and nine a.m., since when it has been quite clear; the temperature of air, which at sunrise was as low as 72°, has reached a maximum of 92°: it is at present 89°, and that of the surface of the water in the creek 78°. Two other thunderstorms have passed over since we have been on the creek, from only one of which we have received any rain worth mentioning.

Most of the rest of this report consisted of observations made with the use of the sextant and other instruments, each of which required experience to understand and handle correctly.

Everyone had calculated that it would be advisable if the entire party remained another four months at Cooper's Creek, until March 1861, when it would be autumn. If they waited until then they could avoid the necessity of travelling during the hot Australian midsummer, when conditions would be very difficult. Yet Burke was impatient to move on; anxious to complete the expedition and keep ahead of his rival Stuart. As a result, he and Wills were becoming increasingly frustrated with Wright's failure to appear. Precious time was slipping away, and they were ever more determined to get to the Gulf of Carpentaria while they still had the opportunity.

The same day as he produced his report, on 15 December, Wills wrote to Bessy again, telling her that they had just moved their quarters to a better site about 20 miles down the creek, and describing heavy thunderstorms towards the north which he hoped would provide them with plenty of water:

> If so, I shall soon be able to send you a good long letter without resorting to the use of a pencil. I wish I could send mamma a few lines, but she must read yours and fancy it written to her: I have not even time to send a line to my father. Tell mamma that I am getting into that robust state of health that I always enjoy when in the bush; a tremendous appetite, and can eat anything. One of our chief articles of consumption is horseflesh: it is very nice; you would scarcely know it from beef.

In his letter Wills also told Bessy that the next day they planned to start for Eyre's Creek, on the way to the Gulf of Carpentaria. It seemed Burke and Wills had finally tired of waiting for Wright and the supplies.

Previously, on 29 October, when their forward party had reached Torowoto Swamp, Burke had sent Wright back to Menindee for the others, giving him instructions to follow them to Cooper's Creek with the remaining camels and supplies as soon as possible. By 16 December Burke was confidently telling the forward party that he expected Wright to arrive any day.

Unbeknown to Burke, Wright was still in Menindee. From 5 November, when he had arrived back from Torowoto Swamp, Wright had apparently been doing nothing. He said he was waiting for an answer to a letter he had sent via the Exploration Committee, but Dr John Macadam, the committee secretary, denied having ever received any such communication. It later transpired that Wright was not even able to write, something of which few, if any, of the expedition were aware until he gave evidence to a committee of inquiry after the expedition on 12 December 1861, almost a year later. Although Burke's instructions for Wright not to delay were quite unambiguous, he did not in fact start until 26 January 1861. When the time came, his answers to the Royal Commission were full of contradictions, and he could give no satisfactory reason for not having started sooner. Dr Wills was later astonished that anyone should have entrusted Wright with such responsibilities at Menindee after knowing so little about him. His most ardent champion in Melbourne was probably Captain Francis Cadell, who had recommended him to the committee, but by October 1960 there was almost no communication between Cadell and Burke.

Confident of Wright's imminent arrival at Cooper's Creek, Burke decided to split the party again. He, Wills, John King, Charley Gray, one horse and six camels would form an exploration party to Carpentaria, while Brahe was placed in charge of the depot on Cooper's Creek with Dost Mahomet, William Patton, Thomas McDonough, six camels and twelve horses. Brahe was under strict orders to remain there in charge until Wright – or someone else duly appointed by the committee – arrived to take command with the remainder of the expedition from Menindee, or until the return of the exploring party from the Gulf of Carpentaria. During the expedition Brahe had been instructed by Wills in the use of the sextant and other instruments, and had made some progress in learning how to do so. In these aspects he was therefore far better qualified, more widely travelled and experienced than the others who had been left with him at Cooper's Creek.

Burke gave Brahe a sealed packet of papers, with instructions to destroy them if he failed to return. Wills left behind a collection of personal papers, as well as his cherished collection of barometers and thermometers so Brahe could keep meteorological records in his absence. It must have been no small personal sacrifice for the second-in-command. Burke had made a personal decision on the amount of rations they would take, and was working on the assumption that they would consume the same amount each day over the planned three months' exploration. This made no allowances for delays or the likelihood of their needing additional food towards the end of the journey; they would undoubtedly be returning in a weaker state than they had been when setting out.

On the morning of 16 December Burke lined up his men to say goodbye, embracing all whom he was leaving behind. All of them were aware of the risks that were being taken, and one cannot but wonder whether any of them had a sixth sense that it was the last time they would ever see each other. Then he and his party – Wills, King, Gray, one horse and six camels – left Cooper's Creek. It is strange that they did not take more horses. As they had been living on horseflesh so much it would have increased their available food, in addition to the facility of carrying burdens. As the animals would probably have to carry water as well, they instead cut their supplies and equipment to the bare minimum. In addition to food they took a few firearms, some spare clothing and a few scientific instruments. They did not even take tents, but a bedroll and a blanket each for shelter. Considering they were embarking on the most demanding part of the journey, it was unfortunate that they were leaving themselves so poorly resourced.

Brahe did as he was asked and remained at Cooper's Creek waiting for Wright for four months. With hindsight, Dr Wills remarked:

> the position was too much for him, and he gave way when a stronger mind might have stood firm. The worst point about him appears to be his want of consistency and miserable prevarication; maybe weakness rather than abso-lute absence of principle, or of any due sense of right or wrong. He was unfit to direct, but he might have been directed.

This judgement is perhaps a little harsh. Burke was blamed for trusting Brahe, but he was almost certainly the most capable of those who remained behind, and there was little choice available. King later told Dr Wills that it was his son's advice to appoint Brahe, and because the imminent arrival of Wright's party from Menindee was considered such a certainty, the appointment was seen only as a temporary one. It has also been said that it might have proved wiser to leave John King behind in charge, and take Brahe to the Gulf of Carpentaria instead. Brahe could travel by compass and observation, which King could not; and one so qualified might be required for the journey.

At around the same time that the expedition split in December, reports from an Adelaide newspaper reached Melbourne to say that John McDouall Stuart had come close to moving in the direction of the Gulf of Carpentaria, but had been driven back by a hostile tribe of aborigines. Although he had been forced to retreat, he planned to start again soon. The committee unanimously decided that Burke should be kept informed if possible and sent a despatch to Swan Hill, where Burke and his party had left on 9 September. From there, police superintendent Mr Forster sent a junior police officer, Trooper Lyons, to try and catch up with the expedi-tion and deliver the news personally to the leader. In Menindee Lyons met Wright, who tried to dissuade him from continuing, but in vain. Lyons was determined, and so Wright sent Alexander McPherson, a saddler, accompa-nied by Dick, a native, to help Lyons track Burke down. Lyons' little party lost their way, however, and were unable to catch up with Burke and Wills. They were rescued six weeks later, having come perilously close to starving to death.

By now Burke's party were experiencing daily temperatures which gener-ally reached 122°F (50°C) in the shade, and when they reached the desert there would be very little shelter from the sun at its fiercest. However, the rest of the elements were on their side, and except for the excessive heat, travelling conditions were satisfactory on the whole. Recent heavy rain meant that water was easy to find, and contrary to expectations, the aborigines were peaceful.

For the next two months, between December 1860 and February 1861, Wills carefully kept a series of field books, or diaries, with concise reports of their progress for most days – with inevitable omissions and intervals of dates not recorded. These were among the papers later recovered and handed over to his father. Some entries, in pencil, were more in the form of notes, with observations and figures to guide him in his mapping. When the maps were accurate, his journal was imperfect, and vice versa.

Burke's own diary consisted of little more than a scrawled list of dates and campsites. As a senior police officer and administrator he had always been impatient with looking after paperwork. He probably felt that Wills was doing a far better job of recording the expedition than he could ever aspire to, and there was nothing to be gained by bothering himself. Nevertheless, when giving evidence to the commission after the expedition's tragic end, Brahe admitted that he had burnt some of Burke's papers in accordance with the latter's instructions. These may have included a diary, although it is extremely unlikely that it would have been anything like as comprehensive as the one kept by Wills.

According to King, in the evidence he gave to a commission of inquiry after the expedition, Wills normally spent an hour or more writing up his notes when they made camp. He always read what he had written aloud to Burke, who always approved and sometimes suggested minor additions. The diary entries were a good indicator of their morale. The more optimistic he (or they) felt, the more expansive and detailed his writing became. Any mood of gloom or despondency was reflected in short perfunctory entries with little more than the date. Or if things were going really badly, there would be silence for several days. Towards the end, days were either lost or muddled as a fight for survival against the odds became the major consideration.

Wills, who had always hated being idle as much as he deplored idleness in others, was constantly busy, and during his waking hours, never at a loss for something to do. When they were not travelling he spent a great deal of time taking meteorological observations, completing scientific records and writing his journal and reports. Once they halted each night, camp was established and King was responsible for looking after the animals, ensuring they were fed and watered, whilst Gray collected wood for the campfire and prepared the evening meal. While supplies lasted, they normally ate salt beef stew with rice and bread, washed down with a cup of tea. After these jobs were done, all of them helped to check the equipment and do any necessary mending and reorganising of the packs. They then laid the beds out ready for the night, and the last job before they retired was to stoke up the campfire to keep the mosquitoes away. Sometimes they were lucky enough to find, or be offered, a place to lay their heads in native huts, or *gunyahs*, but otherwise they slept out under the open sky. At this stage they were by no means short of rations, though the journey was taking them a little longer than expected. Indeed, although they were often surrounded by wild game such as kangaroos, emus, ducks and turkeys, they had no need as yet to shoot them for food.

While Wills had always been good at keeping himself busy, there was nothing in the way of real amusements or any other people with whom they could socialise. Whenever they had been near to towns and villages in the earlier stages of the journey, there were always inns at which they could find like-minded souls with whom to pleasantly pass an hour or so, as well as enjoy some refreshment, but this enjoyable facility was now denied to them.

On 16 December Wills recorded events with his usual meticulous detail:

The horse having been shod and our reports finished, we started at 6.40 a.m. for Eyre's Creek, the party consisting of Mr Burke, myself, King, and Charley, having with us six camels, one horse, and three months' provisions. We followed down the creek to the point where the sandstone ranges cross the creek, and were accompanied to that place by Brahe, who would return to take charge of the depot. Down to this point the banks of the creek are very rugged and stony, but there is a tolerable supply of grass and salt bush in the vicinity. A large tribe of blacks came pestering us to go to their camp and have a dance, which we declined. They were very troublesome, and nothing but the threat to shoot them will keep them away. They are, however, easily frightened; and, although fine-looking men, decidedly not of a warlike disposition. They show the greatest inclination to take whatever they can, but will run no unnecessary risk in so doing. They seldom carry any weapon, except a shield and a large kind of boomerang, which I believe they use for killing rats, etc. Sometimes, but very seldom, they have a large spear; reed spears seem to be quite unknown to them. They are undoubtedly a finer and better-looking race of men than the blacks on the Murray and Darling, and more peaceful; but in other respects I believe they will not compare favourably with them, for from the little we have seen of them, they appear to be mean-spirited and contemptible in every respect.

Less impulsive, Wills was also much better organised than his leader, who would have done well to follow the example of his rival John McDouall Stuart. The Scotsman and his party travelled six days a week, resting on the Sabbath, so as to give themselves and their animals proper rest at regular intervals. During his expeditions, Stuart devised a set of strict rules which served him and his men very well. Among them were instructions that all orders were to be taken from the leader, and in his absence from the second-in-command; that when anything was used, it had to be packed up in the same manner as found and replaced exactly from where it had been taken; when on the march, no water was to be used from their existing supplies without the leader's permission; nobody was allowed to fire on the natives without orders except in self-defence; and each man must sleep with his arms at his side, and in case of attack from the natives, a half-circle must be formed three feet apart. In addition, breakfast always had to be ready at the same time, with half an hour allowed, immediately after which the horses would be prepared for the day's travel. Each horse and pack-saddle was numbered, and they were divided into groups, lined up every morning and evening in the same order so that all equipment could be located at once.

Such rules ensured that his expeditions were well-paced and ran smoothly with the minimum of discord or argument. From what is known of Wills, and how meticulously he kept his instruments and materials, it is quite likely that if he had been given a free hand he would have devised something similar, whereas Burke was too ready to leave things to chance.

During the next few days the expedition travelled, on average, 15 miles per day. On 19 December Wills noted:

the ground was very bad for travelling on, being much cracked up and intersected by innumerable channels, which continually carried off the water of a large creek. Some of the valleys beyond this were very pretty, the ground being sound and covered with fresh plants, which made them look beautifully green.

Their main priority was to look for water supplies, and that same day their attention was attracted by various birds, including red-breasted cockatoos, pigeons and a crow. Their presence made them sure that there was water nearby, but their hopes were soon destroyed on discovering a claypan drying up, containing only enough liquid to make the clay boggy. A little later their luck turned, and they came across a creek with 'two or three waterholes of good milky water' where they decided they would camp for the night.

Next day they did not leave until half-past eight in the morning, 'having delayed to refill the water-bags with the milky water, which all of us found to be a great treat again. It is certainly more pleasant to drink than the clear water, and at the same time more satisfying.' Spirits were high as they travelled north-west by north, their course taking them 'through some pretty country, lightly timbered and well grassed', as they saw the line of creek timber winding through the valley on their left. A little further on they came within sight of a large lagoon, followed by a creek, beside which they decided would be the site of the next camp. This area contained plentiful supplies of water, and large numbers of several species of wildfowl. 'It is very shallow, but is surrounded by the most pleasing woodland scenery, and everything in the vicinity looks fresh and green.' In addition they found a camp of about fifty aborigines nearby, who brought them a new delicacy in the form of presents of cooked fish, in return for which the explorers gave them some beads and matches:

> These fish we found to be a most valuable addition to our rations. They were of the same kind as we had found elsewhere, but finer, being from nine to ten inches long, and two to three inches deep, and in such good condition that they might have been fried in their own fat. It is a remarkable fact, that these were the first blacks who have offered us any fish since we reached Cooper's Creek.

On 21 December they left their camp at five-thirty in the morning, and tried to persuade one or two of the aborigines to go with them, but without success. They were rewarded with another day of satisfactory travel, and they camped at another 'splendid waterhole'. At this point the creek flowed north:

> through a large lightly timbered flat, on which it partially runs out. The ground is, however, sound and well clothed with grass and salsolaceous plants. Up to this point the country through which we have passed has been of the

finest description for pastoral purposes. The grass and saltbush are everywhere abundant, and water is plentiful with every appearance of permanence.

Later that week, at an oasis called Gray's Creek, they allowed themselves a day of rest in order to celebrate Christmas – albeit in surely the least festive setting imaginable to Englishmen:

> This was doubly pleasant, as we had never, in our most sanguine moments, anticipated finding such a delightful oasis in the desert. Our camp was really an agreeable place, for we had all the advantages of food and water, attending a position of a large creek or river, and were at the same time free from the annoyance of the numberless ants, flies, and mosquitoes that are invariably met with amongst timber or heavy scrub.

Wills' diary entries for the next few days followed a similar pattern, with detailed references to early morning departures, supplies of water or lack of it, the lay of the land, birds and vegetation. There were occasional casualties among his equipment; one of his spare thermometers was broken, and the glass of his aneroid barometer cracked when a camel rolled on it while the pack was on its back. A typical entry, from 9 January, talks about walking 6 miles of undulating plains, covered with rich vegetation:

> Several ducks rose from the little creeks as we passed, and flocks of pigeons were flying in all directions. The richness of the vegetation is evidently not suddenly arising from chance thunderstorms, for the trees and bushes on the open plain are everywhere healthy and fresh looking; very few dead ones are to be seen; besides which, the quantity of dead and rotten grass which at present almost overpowers in some places the young blades shows that this is not the first crop of the kind.

Next day, they left camp at 5.20 a.m. 'with a full supply of water, determined to risk no reverses, and to make a good march'. During the night, Wills noted they had 'been nearly deafened by the noise of the cicadariae, and but for our large fires should have been kept awake all night by the mosquitoes'. On 11 January there was a new experience for them:

> in the excitement of exploring fine well-watered country, forgot all about the eclipse of the sun until the reduced temperature and peculiarly gloomy

appearance of the sky drew our attention to the matter; it was then too late to remedy the deficiency, so we made a good day's journey, the moderation of the midday heat, which was only about 86 degrees, greatly assisting us.

Two days later, they encountered a new problem. The lush grasslands had been ideal for travelling, but now they came across small but sharp and hostile outcrops of stone, which meant they had to work to protect the camels' feet. That morning they were delayed in leaving camp by having to spend longer than anticipated trying to get the shoes on the animals, 'a matter in which we were eminently unsuccessful'. They had their breakfast before starting, for almost the first time since leaving the depot, and after crossing the creek they continued due north until coming into sight of the range ahead, when they took a north–half-east direction in order to clear the eastern front of it. For the next week they found the going difficult, and Wills' diary was uncharacteristically empty for a few days whilst they navigated a route which took them over sharp ridges and steep slopes, with the camels sweating from fear and bleeding and groaning.

To add to their difficulties, Burke and Wills were aware that they had entered the territory of the Kalkadoons, one of the indigenous tribes. It was evident that they were watching the explorers with grave suspicion. Some twenty years later, miners prospecting in the area for copper learnt that the Kalkadoons – who soon became notorious for their unfriendliness and guerrilla campaigns against those they saw as invaders – had wanted to ambush and kill the explorers, but were put off by the 'giant roaring beasts' (the camels) whom they assumed must be supernatural, so they retreated to higher ground.

Meanwhile, still in Menindee, Wright was busy purchasing pack animals and saddles, but as the station owners knew he was desperate enough to pay almost any price asked for them, they pitched their demands accordingly. This, the time taken to train them, plus a lack of communication from both the committee and Burke and Wills, resulted in endless procrastinating, aided by the lack of any pressure to come to a decision. Eventually William Hodgkinson, previously of the *Melbourne Weekly Age*, decided he would have to take matters into his own hands. On 22 December he wrote out a despatch dictated by Wright, advising the committee as a body of the reason for their not having yet embarked. It reached Melbourne nine days later.

While the members of the committee, Secretary Dr Macadam in particular, were surprised to hear that there had been any delay, they called an emergency meeting at which they confirmed Wright as third-in-command, and voted him an additional £400 for purchasing more horses and saddles. Having delivered the letter personally to John Macadam on New Year's Eve, Hodgkinson was back at Menindee by 9 January 1861, whereupon they set about buying more animals, organising stores and finalising other preparations. The party, consisting of Becker, Dr Beckler, Charles Stone, John Smith, William Purcell and Belooch, left on 26 January. On 12 February they reached the halfway mark between Menindee and Cooper's Creek – Torowoto Swamp – where they stopped for two days' rest. They were now effectively four months behind Wills and Burke, who had been here in October 1860.

Over a period of several days Burke and Wills made what they felt was disappointingly slow progress. However, by 27 January they had succeeded in crossing the inhospitable Selwyn Ranges, and the land ahead of them was more flat. By the end of the month, they had crossed Augustus Charles Gregory's east–west track across the top end of Australia, and were about 120 miles from the coast.[2] By doing so, according to the instructions which the committee had issued Burke, they had completed their official responsibility to explore the country between Augustus Gregory's track and Cooper's Creek, and they were now halfway through their own predetermined schedule of three months. They were by now also using up their food supplies more quickly than anticipated, and every day they continued further north would mean less rations for the return journey.

Had they turned round at this point to make the journey back to Melbourne, which they were perfectly entitled to do, they would have undoubtedly entered the city and been greeted as heroes. Yet Burke's obstinacy and determination to continue against the odds proved their undoing. He vowed that he was going to reach the Gulf of Carpentaria, even if he got there without the shirt on his back. The more cautious, prudent Wills probably appreciated the danger they faced, and one cannot but wonder whether he tried to impress such views on Burke. But ever the loyal lieutenant, if he tried to argue his point and failed to reach agreement, he accepted his leader's decision as final and silently acquiesced.

This fateful decision coincided with what was perhaps the worst time of year: the few weeks prior to the season of heavy rainfall, with intense humidity which made it difficult to breathe. Sweating profusely, they suffered almost continuously from headaches and lethargy. Temperatures remained very high at night, the air was alive with mosquitoes, the atmosphere was muggy and sleep was almost impossible. To make matters worse, food rotted quickly and the animals' leather harnesses were particularly susceptible to mould.

Having struggled over the Selwyn Ranges, the six camels suffered most of all. On 30 January they started at half-past seven in the morning after several abortive attempts to get one of the animals out of the soft bed of the creek. Wills thought they should try and bring him down the creek until they found a place where he could easily get out and on to dry land, but after they had gone 2–3 miles to look for such a spot, 'it was found necessary to leave him behind, as it was almost impossible to get him through some of the waterholes, and had separated King from the party, which became a matter for very serious consideration when we found blacks hiding in the box trees close to us'.

The ground had become so boggy after days and nights of heavy rain that all the remaining camels were finding it increasingly difficult, too. Burke decided it was hopeless to try to take them any further north, so he ordered King and Gray to stay at their current base with the camels, while he and Wills continued on foot towards the shore of Carpentaria, taking it in turns with the horse. On 10 February they started out after breakfast with only three days' rations.[3] For part of the journey they passed alongside a river, which Burke said he proposed to name after his old friend Lord Cloncurry, whom he had known in Ireland.

As they were crossing the creek, the horse became bogged down in a quicksand, and both men only succeeded in extricating him by undermining him on the creek's side and then lugging him into the water. Once they had done so, they found most of the land was so soft and rotten that even with only a saddle and 25lbs on his back, the animal was having great difficulty in walking. After another 5 miles he became trapped in a small creek, and when they got him out a second time he seemed so weak that they had their doubts as to how much further he would be able to go. Fortunately, they found some better ground near the water's edge, which led them to a hard, well-worn path, and then to a forest where the aborigines had been digging yams around their campfires. There were so many yams that only the best had been taken and there were plenty of perfectly satisfactory rejects for the two explorers to collect and eat. About half a mile further on, they came across an aborigine man, woman and child. They stopped to take out some of the pistols on the horse, close enough for the man to see them. He looked in their direction, stared, signalled to several others who had gathered around, and they 'shuffled off in the quietest manner possible'.

Wills recorded that nearby was a hut, looking out on an extensive marsh, where large flocks of wild geese, plover and pelicans were feeding. As the explorers continued along their way, they came to a channel of water and passed three more aborigines, who helpfully pointed out to them the best way to proceed through the boggy area ahead. They walked on a further 3 miles and then camped for the night.

Although they had stopped on the upper tidal reaches of an estuary, they were unsure precisely where they were. Wills had plotted their journey towards the Albert River, which was 100km west, but they were actually camped by the Little Bynoe River, an arm of the River Flinders. Maybe instinct told them that this was as far north as they were likely to reach. On the following morning they considered trying to get to the shore of the northern coast which overlooked the Gulf of Carpentaria, but swamps and severe floods were blocking their way onto the shore, and it was raining very hard. The horse was by now 'completely baked', and they began to take seriously the fact that they had only brought three days' rations with them. Their total provisions were also running out fast, with only enough left for twenty-seven days, at which point they would need to replenish from supplies at Cooper's Creek. Yet they were fifty-nine days away from Cooper's Creek.

Nevertheless, they were tantalisingly close. Uncharacteristically, Wills left no written record of his feelings at this stage, and this time it was Burke who summed up their thoughts, albeit briefly, in his notebook. 'It would have been well to say that we reached the sea,' he wrote, 'but we could not obtain a view of the open ocean, although we made every effort to do so.'[4] Though it may have been a mild disappointment not to go, literally, the extra mile, they had succeeded in crossing the continent from south to north, the first Europeans to accomplish such a feat. At daybreak, they turned back to rejoin Gray and King. It was vital that they did so before using up their remaining rations.

1. William John Wills.

2. Bridge Street, Ipplepen: the village where the family moved to from Totnes in 1845. (© Totnes Image Bank and Rural Archive)

3. A nineteenth-century reconstruction of the schoolroom at Ashburton as it would have been when William John Wills was a pupil. (© Totnes Image Bank and Rural Archive)

4. A detail from the desk at Ashburton School on which Wills carved his name. (© Mike Wills)

5. Bayard's Cove, Dartmouth, where William John Wills and Tom Wills sailed for Australia in 1852. (© Totnes Image Bank and Rural Archive)

6. Melbourne Harbour, *c.* 1860–70.

7. A Moreton Bay fig tree, planted by Burke and Wills when they stopped at Swan Hill in September 1860. (© Mike Wills)

8. Cooper's Creek, where the expedition first arrived in November 1860. (© Mike Wills)

9. Burke and Wills during the last days of the expedition, from a drawing by an unknown artist, *c.* 1920. (© Patrick Harrison Collection)

10. Burke, Wills and King in the desert during the latter stages of their journey, from an engraving by Nicholas Chevalier, 1868.

11. The funeral procession of Burke and Wills passing the Haymarket Theatre, Bourne Street, Melbourne, on 21 January 1863. (© Patrick Harrison Collection)

12. The memorial at Swan Hill, with its inscription recording the departure of Burke and Wills and their expedition on 12 September 1860, unveiled in 1914. (© Mike Wills)

13. The Wills memorial, a granite obelisk at The Plains, Totnes, opposite the house where he had been born, unveiled in 1864. (© Russ Parkin)

14. The medallion showing Wills' profile, added to the memorial at Totnes in 1893. (© Kim Van der Kiste)

15. *Left:* The statue commemorating Burke and Wills, Melbourne, by Charles Summers, unveiled in 1864. (© Dave Phoenix)

16. *Below:* The gravestone of Burke and Wills, Melbourne General Cemetery. (© Mike Wills)

17. *Below:* The title page and dedication of Dr Wills' book based on his son's letters and diaries, published in 1863. (© Mike Wills)

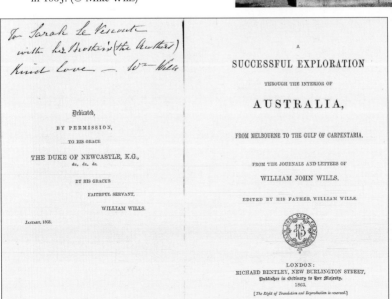

A

SUCCESSFUL EXPLORATION

THROUGH THE INTERIOR OF

AUSTRALIA,

FROM MELBOURNE TO THE GULF OF CARPENTARIA.

FROM THE JOURNALS AND LETTERS OF

WILLIAM JOHN WILLS.

EDITED BY HIS FATHER, WILLIAM WILLS.

LONDON:
RICHARD BENTLEY, NEW BURLINGTON STREET,
Publisher in Ordinary to Her Majesty.
1863.
[*The Right of Translation and Reproduction is reserved.*]

To Sarah le Vescomte
with her Brother's (the Author's)
kind love — Wm Wills

Dedicated,

BY PERMISSION,

TO HIS GRACE

THE DUKE OF NEWCASTLE, K.G.,
&c., &c., &c.

BY HIS GRACE'S

FAITHFUL SERVANT,

WILLIAM WILLS.

JANUARY, 1863.

6

Return to Cooper's Creek

Burke and Wills rejoined Gray and King on 12 February. Since leaving Cooper's Creek on 16 December they had got through more than two-thirds of their supply of rations. Now they were left with 83lb of flour, 3lb of pork, 25lb of dried meat, 12lb of biscuit and 12lb of rice, or just one month's worth of provisions – about half of what they required to retrace the journey that had taken them fifty-nine days. Clearly, Burke had not anticipated any delays in their outward journey when organising rations. Their diets were supplemented by portulac, or common purslane, a plant with fleshy leaves which flowered in the rainy season, and this became their principal ration when boiled, described by Wills as 'an excellent vegetable'. In addition they still managed to catch fish and shoot ducks, crows and hawks. As a last resort, if matters were to become really desperate, they still had a source of meat in their six remaining animals, and in Golah, the camel they had left behind.

Ahead of them was a distance of 700 miles back to the depot at Cooper's Creek, and the outward journey had seen them manage between 12 and 15 miles a day. Now the animals' loads were lighter, and since they had become familiar with the route, they hoped they would be able to travel more quickly. Apart from Gray, who was complaining of headaches, they all appeared reasonably fit. The animals would have undoubtedly benefited from more rest, but the shortage of rations made it imperative that they keep going without delay. In order to preserve their dwindling stocks, Burke decided to limit them to a daily amount of twelve dried sticks of meat and ¼lb of flour.

Before leaving their camp, King and Gray cut the initial B on a few small trees, and buried a cache of equipment and books, accompanied by a note of explanation.

On 13 February, after only one day of rest, they set out again in heavy rain. Instead of feeling exhilarated, or at least sustained by the achievement of having reached the north coast and accomplishing the full first stage of their mission, they were tired and weary, their morale clearly ebbing. For the next stage of the journey the entries in Wills' diary were much shorter and more to the point than those he had made over the previous few weeks. Sometimes they comprised of nothing more than the date and the name of the camp where they pitched. Torrential rain was turning the ground into a quagmire and slowing them down considerably, and as they had no tents, they were faced with no alternative but to sleep in the open and the wet. One of the more expansive entries in Wills' diary, for 21 February, reads:

> Between four and five o'clock a heavy thunderstorm broke over us, having given very little warning of its approach. There had been lightning and thunder towards the south-east and south ever since noon yesterday. The rain was incessant and very heavy for an hour and a half, which made the ground so boggy that the animals could scarcely walk over it; we nevertheless started at ten minutes to seven a.m., and after floundering along for half an hour halted for breakfast. We then moved on again, but soon found that the travelling was too heavy for the camels, so camped for the remainder of the day. In the afternoon the sky cleared a little, and the sun soon dried the ground, considering. Shot a pheasant, and much disappointed at finding him all feathers and claws. This bird nearly resembles a cock pheasant in plumage, but in other respects it bears more the character of the magpie or crow; the feathers are remarkably wiry and coarse.

The following evening they had another 'fearful thunderstorm', with flashes of lightning 'so vivid and incessant as to keep up a continual light for short intervals, overpowering the moonlight', accompanied by heavy rain and strong squalls lasting over an hour. 'The sky remained overcast for the rest of the night, and the following morning was both sultry and oppressive, with the ground so boggy as to be almost impassable.' King and Gray were now both suffering from headaches and back pain. Wills, who had been the most physically fit of them all, was beginning to feel the strain as well. On 23 February he noted it was a fine day; they had crossed a creek and halted for the day on a patch of comparatively dry ground near the river. At the end of the day they found somewhere to camp for the night, and Wills recorded:

> the evening was most oppressively hot and sultry, so much so that the slightest exertion made one feel as if he were in a state of suffocation. The dampness of the atmosphere prevented any evaporation, and gave one a helpless feeling of lassitude that I have never before experienced to such an extent. All the party complained of the same symptoms, and the horses [sic] showed distinctly the effect of the evening trip, short as it was.

Half an hour after they had turned in, it began to rain, but after the clouds moved on and the sky cleared, 'the atmosphere became rather cooler and less sultry, so that, with the assistance of a little smoke to keep the mosquitoes off, we managed to pass a tolerable night'.

Back at Cooper's Creek, Brahe and the others had been cutting timber to build a stockade around the camp. A solid palisade of saplings driven firmly into the ground, covering an area of about 18–20ft, it enclosed the tent Burke had left behind plus their supplies of firearms and ammunition. Tents were set up outside the stockade, by the cooking fires and the area where the twelve horses and six camels were tied up every night. The abundant supply of rats was proving a mixed blessing; provisions had to be hung up in the trees to keep them safe, but the animals, being easy to catch and cook, provided a ready supply of meat.

The men had to be constantly on their guard against pilfering by the aborigines, and somebody needed to keep watch around the clock. On a couple of occasions Brahe was obliged to fire a shot over their heads to deter them from coming too close. Early in January, when a party entered the camp by daylight, he seized one of the men and pushed him over. The tribe ran away but returned later, some of them armed with spears and boomerangs, their faces and bodies painted in a sign of war. Brahe walked out to meet them, drew a large circle around the camp and then indicated by signs that if any of them crossed the line, he would not hesitate to fire. Some men crossed the line in a challenge, to which Brahe shot his gun off into the tree and the tribe took to their heels again.

Although there was plenty to be done, one cannot avoid the feeling that it must have been a very monotonous existence for them at times. They probably spent more time than they would have liked just drinking tea from their dwindling supplies as they sat gazing at the campfire. They only had their own company, with no amusements to while away the time or provide relief from the drudgery of their mission. Watching spectacular dawns and sunsets, or observing changes in the wildlife, the weather and the land were the nearest to excitement they had.

The three-month waiting period which had been mutually agreed would have taken them up to mid-March. Brahe was expecting Burke and Wills to rejoin them at around that time, although he was prepared to wait a little longer – until the start of May if necessary. Of more concern than Burke and Wills not returning on schedule was Wright's failure to make any appearance at all. Wright had turned back from Torowoto Swamp at the end of October, on the understanding that he would bring back the bulk stores to Cooper's Creek as soon as possible. By March, there was not only no sign of him, but also no news as to his whereabouts.

Around 24 March the temperature suddenly dropped after having been around 112°F (44°C) in the shade. The nights became very cold and there was thunder and lightning with strong winds. Although most of their food supplies were holding out well, they had no dried fruit or vegetables. Early in April William Patton, the blacksmith, began to complain that he was unwell and suffering from sore gums. On 4 April he collapsed; his legs and arms were swollen and his mouth was so sore he could not eat and had to be put to bed, where he became progressively more feeble. Brahe and Thomas McDonough both began to suffer similar symptoms, although less severely, and their ankles became swollen every time they mounted a horse.

It was now four months since Burke, Wills and the others had gone, a month longer than they had planned to be away. Sometimes Brahe rode out to the hills around the creek, looking alternately south-east for any sign of Wright, or north for the others. Although he had not been left any written instructions, Burke had told him that if they were not back at the depot within three months, Brahe was at liberty to consider him 'perished'.

Though Brahe was prepared to wait longer, the ill-health of the men gave them a further reason not to extend their period of waiting by too long. By 18 April, he had made up his mind that they were going to leave on the Sunday, three days later. The ailing Patton was desperate to go back to Menindee for medical attention, and the longer they stayed where they were, the greater the chances that he would die. The others were increasingly weak and undernourished, and it was a strain even looking after the animals. As every day that went by meant less chance of Burke returning, it seemed there was nothing to be gained by prolonging their time there. Brahe ordered Patton to shoe the horses, and it proved to be the last task the dying blacksmith was able to perform before he collapsed. By the following day, he was unable to move and had to lie there helplessly as the others packed up their things and tidied the camp. The next two days were spent preparing to leave. Brahe cut a message into a tree, called McDonough as a witness, took out Burke's letters and, in accordance with the instructions he had been left, set fire to them.

Meanwhile, back in Melbourne, nothing had been heard from or about the expedition since October, when the group first split and Burke departed with a forward party from Menindee for Cooper's Creek. The members of the Royal Society were, however, sure all was well and did not even meet in January 1861. They met twice in February to audit their finances and seemed convinced that no news was good news, certain of their superiority over Stuart's expedition and confident that Burke and Wills would soon return safely. The press had voiced its fears that after Landells' resignation the expedition was in grave danger of fragmenting or dispersing, as if they expected the leaders to admit failure and return at any time. However, when the journalists heard in October that Burke and Wills were now leading a smaller, more compact party towards Cooper's Creek, they took it as a sign that all must be well.

The one person who had his doubts was Dr Wills. By March he was sufficiently concerned to suggest that it was time a rescue party was sent in search of them. Most of the committee regarded him as an interfering busybody who did not know when to let well alone. None of them, it is unnecessary to state, had a much-loved, conscientious and hardworking son with a brilliant future in front of him, whose whereabouts was unknown and whose life could be at grave risk. At the beginning of the month he wrote of his fears to Professor Neumayer at the observatory, whom he was sure would have his son's best interests at heart.

The latter replied on 8 March that while he could obviously not give a definite answer as to the men's safety, he was sure the party must have reached the Gulf of Carpentaria by then. It was his belief that they had not only already arrived there, but moreover, assuming that everything had gone according to plan after leaving Cooper's Creek, they would also have recrossed much of the desert country. Although Neumayer had his concerns about the Exploration Committee's management of the expedition, he stated that he personally had every confidence in the 'character and energy' of William John Wills, and was sure they would succeed:

> I cannot help regretting that the Committee should not have understood the force of my arguments, when I advised them to send the expedition towards the north-west. This would very likely have forwarded the task considerably. My feeling is not very strong as to the results we may expect from the present attempt. Indeed, as far as science and practical advantages are concerned, I look upon the whole as a mistake. Mr Wills is entirely alone; he has no one to assist him in his zeal, and take a part of his onerous duties from him. Had he been put in a position to make valuable magnetic observations, he would have earned the thanks of the scientific world. But, under existing circumstances, he can do nothing at all for the advancement of this particular branch. However, I hope future expeditions will afford him an opportunity to fill up that deficiency, if he should now be successful. The affair with Landells was nothing more nor less than what I expected and was quite prepared to hear. The man was not more qualified for the task he undertook than he would have been for any scientific position in the expedition. I am confident Mr Wills is all right, and that Mr Burke and he will agree well together.

However, Dr Wills was not completely alone in his concerns. He had an ally in William Lockhart-Morton, an amateur explorer who had applied for leadership of the expedition but was never seriously considered by the committee. Maybe he had an axe to grind, but he also thought the members were being unnecessarily complacent in their *laissez-faire* attitude. In a letter published in the *Melbourne Argus*, he asked what had become of the expedition. 'Surely the committee,' he wrote, 'are not alive to the necessity of sending some one up? Burke has by this time crossed the continent, or is lost. What has become of Wright? What is he doing?'

By April the *Melbourne Argus* was adding its voice to the growing public campaign which called for a relief party to be sent out to look for the missing men, castigating the committee for its inaction and pointing out that people were losing confidence in its management abilities, such as they were. Neumayer rose stoutly to the Society's defence; while he conceded that it was odd nothing had been heard from Burke or Wills, he still believed that all was well and that there was absolutely no need to send out any rescue parties.

By the end of February, Burke, Wills, Gray and King were falling some way behind their target speed of 12 miles per day. On 2 March they were reunited with Golah the camel, who had now become little more than a living skeleton:

> He looks thin and miserable; seems to have fretted a great deal, probably at finding himself left behind, and he has been walking up and down our tracks till he has made a regular pathway; could find no sign of his having been far off, although there is a splendid feed to which he could have gone. He began to eat as soon as he saw the other camels.

But Golah proved too ill to be able to make a proper recovery, and he had become far too weak to keep up with the party any longer. Four days later, they had to abandon him to his fate in the bush. Whether they did not shoot Golah out of sentiment or because he was too thin to yield much meat, Wills' diary did not record.

Burke had devised what he considered was a fair way of dividing their precious dwindling rations. At every meal, he served food out onto four numbered plates which he covered with a towel. The others stood with their backs turned, called a number, and each was then handed the plate corresponding to the number they had called.

That same week, Gray rode over an object which they thought at first glance must be a log – until he struck it with a stirrup iron. Weighing over 11lb, it turned out to be the largest snake they had ever seen in the wild, measuring 8ft 4in in length and 7in in girth. It retained this same thickness from its head to within 20in of the tail, before tapering rapidly. From the tip of the nose to 5in back, the neck was black above and below, the rest being yellow with irregular brown transverse bars on a yellowish-brown ground. It did not seem to have poisonous fangs, only two distinct rows of teeth in each jaw, and two small claws of nails, just under half an inch long, one on each side of the vent. It looked like too good a delicacy to cast aside, so they cooked it for their supper.

On the following day Burke complained of severe dysentery, and said he felt giddy. He managed, with difficulty, to mount his horse, but was unable to keep himself in the seat. For two days he reluctantly and slowly dragged himself along on foot. By 7 March he was reasonably fit and well again, whereas Gray had caught cold 'through carelessness in covering himself'. He was becoming weaker, barely strong enough to do anything of importance. Wills recorded that the other three thought he was 'gammoning', or trying to evade his fair share of the work.

On 25 March, after several weeks of reasonable progress, they started out at half-past five in the morning. Wills took some time-altitudes after they had eaten breakfast and was about to return to the previous camp for some items which had been left behind, when he found Gray hiding behind a tree, furtively helping himself to skilligolee, or gruel. When Wills angrily asked him what he thought he was doing, Gray said shamefacedly that he had taken it without permission because he was suffering from dysentery. Furious that one of the team should have let them down and shown such a lack of self-discipline, Wills told him sharply to report himself to Burke. Frightened of the Irishman's fiery temper, Gray begged King to go and tell him instead.

This had the unfortunate effect of making Burke even more angry, and he gave Gray 'a good thrashing'. What was exactly meant by this has been open to endless speculation ever since. Whether the Irishman actually hit Gray or boxed him on the ears is in doubt, and King later suggested that the punishment was merely 'six or seven slaps on the ear'. Yet the fact remains that any mutual trust had now been shattered. Wills noted that in the last few days some of their supplies had 'been found to run unaccountably short', and Gray was held responsible. He even took it upon himself to examine some of Gray's stools, to see whether it really was dysentery or whether the man was making feeble excuses for his behaviour. As a result, Gray was relieved of his responsibility for the stores.

From then on, the atmosphere was noticeably strained. A further lack of morale was reflected in Wills' subsequent diary entries; he noted how the areas they were crossing, formerly fresh-looking and green, were now completely dried up. Stretches of stony countryside proved even more exhausting than ever as the jagged edges underfoot tore at their already badly worn boots. One night they found themselves in the middle of a fierce dust storm, and again, with no tents in which to seek shelter, they were reduced to sleeping in the open. Next morning they had to dig themselves out of the sand.

On 30 March Boocha, one of the remaining camels, was killed. They spent the day cutting him up and jerking him: cutting the meat into strips and laying it out in the sun to dry. The weather conditions were improving slightly – apart from the days when cyclonic storms blowing with rain or red dust prevented them from continuing. On 8 April Wills noted in his diary that the creek contained more water, and there was a considerable quantity of green grass in its bed, though it was still much dried up in comparison to when they had passed it the first time. He recorded that young grass and portulac leaves were growing in the flats and on the sides of the sand ridges. And a less cheerful, more cynical note was added about Gray, 'who pretended that he could not walk', and complained pathetically of weakness in his legs and back. Only a month earlier, the others might have had some sympathy for him, but the matter of his helping himself to extra rations had cost him dearly.

On 10 April, as they reached the Diamantina River, it was time for their horse to be sacrificed. He was utterly worn out, and his legs buckled as he sank feebly into the sand. To the sentimental Burke it was a terrible wrench to despatch a faithful friend who had endured so much with them, who had carried him across so much of the continent; but Wills was more matter-of-fact as he noted that the animal was:

> so reduced and knocked up for want of food that there appeared little chance of his reaching the other side of the desert; and as we were running short of food of every description ourselves, we thought it best to secure his flesh at once. We found it healthy and tender, but without the slightest trace of any fat in any portion of the body.

They spent the day cutting him up and jerking his meat. By this time Burke's party was getting weaker; unable to carry more than a light pack each, and with fewer pack animals to carry things, they were regularly discarding any equipment which they felt was not strictly necessary. One day towards the end of March they discarded about 60lb of luggage, hanging it from the branches of a tree so they could go back and reclaim it at a later date if possible.

On 15 April Gray was too exhausted to support himself on horseback, and had to be strapped to the saddle. Even as he weakened visibly he had still not been forgiven for taking the food, and the normally easy-going Wills was coldly judgemental about the man who had been a former comrade but had betrayed their trust. He suspected Gray might have been an alcoholic and believed that the man's constitution 'was gone through drink, as he had lived in a public house at Swan Hill, and I have heard since that he drunk very heavily there'. Little did he know that Gray was genuinely very ill. Later that day he became delirious, and lost the power of speech.

By 17 April the expedition had reached Polygonum Swamp, 15 miles from Cooper's Creek. Early in the morning they found Gray dead in his bedroll. 'He had not spoken a word distinctly since his first attack, which was just as we were about to start', Wills noted, perhaps with a pang of conscience. Until his transgression, he had been referred to in the diaries as Charley, but after that the name was always Gray. Burke gave the order for them to halt, and King took a shovel and spent several hours scraping a hole large enough to bury what was left of Gray's emaciated corpse in his flannel trousers, short-sleeved shirt and hat. They dispensed with anything approaching even an improvised burial service, but on the grave they placed some unwanted camel pads, and hung a rifle on a tree which stood above it. Afterwards they abandoned more of their equipment. Wills had gradually shed most of his beloved instruments, which he had collected and cared for so painstakingly. It was a wrench to have to do so, but he still held on doggedly to his field books and diaries.

On 18 April they set out again, carrying a little dried meat, a couple of spades, the remaining firearms and a few camel pads for bedding. Although he was not noted for his magnanimity to the natives, Burke had been very generous in giving away their spare shirts to them. Now they were in desperate need of new clothes and boots, as what they were wearing was very thin and threadbare. Indeed, they were so cold when they lay down to sleep that they had to try and keep a fire burning throughout the night.

Two days later, on 20 April, they carried on, with Burke riding one camel, while Wills and King took it in turns on the other. They divided their remaining provisions and ate them all except for the last pound and a half of dried meat. Burke and Wills both knew that they would need all their remaining strength to complete the final days' travel back to Cooper's Creek, where they were sure they would be reunited with the others. Only this vision - the knowledge of further supplies, a good rest in comfortable conditions and the companionship of the others which they had so missed during the last four months – drove the men on despite their diminishing energies. As they staggered onwards they were sustained above all by the thought that once arrived at Cooper's Creek, it would then only be a few weeks before they returned to Melbourne to be welcomed as heroes.

At Cooper's Creek, at about half-past ten on the morning of 21 April, Brahe, McDonough, Dost Mahomet and the ailing Patton – who was beyond recovery and would be dead within six weeks – had given up all hope of Burke and Wills returning. Having packed everything up, they took a final look around the depot to make sure they were leaving nothing of importance behind them. They then mounted their horses and camels, and left.

In the final stages of their return journey to Cooper's Creek, Burke, Wills, King and their last two remaining camels had missed Brahe by one day. As the moon was coming up Burke rode on ahead, telling the others that he was sure he could see the tents, convinced he could make out the shadowy forms of Brahe, McDonough and Patton waiting for them. Drawing ever closer, he called out their names, one by one. There was no answer.

7

Into the Final Sleep

Riding into the depot camp at Cooper's Creek on the evening of 21 April, Wills and Burke were astonished to see the place completely deserted. There were piles of ashes left from the old campfires, and a few pieces of abandoned equipment. At first they thought the base camp must have moved a little further down the creek, just out of sight. Although exhausted from their journey, they decided to continue a short distance further to find them. Then, on the banks of the waterhole, Wills noticed a freshly carved inscription on a coolibah tree:

DIG
UNDER
3 FT NW

On a branch nearby was the date, 21 April 1861. King checked the ashes of the campfires and found they were still warm – Brahe and the rest of the party had left just a few hours earlier. Burke had asked them to wait for thirteen weeks, and they had waited eighteen. Brahe's buried note explained that the party had left only about nine hours previously, leaving some food beneath a coolibah tree in the event of their return, and carving a message in the bark to mark the spot.

Wills and King paced out a distance from the tree to a place where they could see the earth had recently been turned over. After digging down several inches, they found the box containing the rest of the rations, and a bottle containing a message written in pencil, signed by Brahe. Dated earlier that day, it read:

> The depot party of the V.E.E. [Victorian Exploring Expedition] leaves this camp today to return to the Darling. I intend to go SE from Camp LX, to get into our old track near Bulloo. Two of my companions and myself are quite well; the third – Patton – has been unable to walk for the last eighteen days, as his leg has been severely hurt when thrown by one of the horses. No person has been up here from the Darling.
>
> We have six camels and twelve horses in good working order.

Burke, who was particularly overwrought, flung himself on the ground and cried. Once they had had time to consider the situation more calmly, their initial impulse was to try and catch up with the other men. Burke asked Wills and King whether they felt they could continue through the night, but they said they were too exhausted, and he agreed. If Brahe's camels and horses were still fit, they would be a long way ahead – too far, in fact. That they should have thrown this last chance away by deciding not to exert themselves any further was ample proof of how physically weak the journey had left them. After four months' arduous travel, they found it an effort to walk more than a few yards at a time. 'Such a leg-bound feeling I never before experienced, and hope I never shall again,' Wills noted. 'The exertion required to get up a piece stretch of rising ground, even without any load, induces an indescribable sensation of pain and helplessness, and the general lassitude makes one unfit for anything.' Only now did he realise what Gray must have suffered when the others thought he was malingering, and he considered it fortunate that the symptoms which had affected him did not come on them 'until we were reduced to an exclusively animal diet of such an inferior description as that offered by the flesh of a worn-out and exhausted horse'. Ironically, they realised that had they not lost a day by staying behind to bury Gray, they would have arrived that vital day earlier.

Fortunately, noted Wills, they had been left 'ample provisions to take us to the bounds of civilization', namely 50lb of flour, 20lb of rice, 60lb of oatmeal, 60lb of sugar and 15lb of dried meat. Apart from this, only a few horse shoes and nails, 'and some odds and ends', were still there. No clothes had been left and their flannel shirts and trousers were fast wearing out; they were reduced to patching them with old horse blankets. King had to crawl on his hands and knees to get to the creek with a billycan and fill it. Making the best of a grim situation, they prepared themselves some supper of oatmeal porridge and sugar. Wills wrote:

> This, together with the excitement of finding ourselves in such a peculiar and most unexpected position had a wonderful effect in removing the stiffness from our legs. Whether it is possible that the vegetables can have so affected us, I know not; but both Mr Burke and I remarked a most decided relief and a strength in the legs greater than we had had for several days. I am inclined to think that but for the abundance of portulac that we obtained on the journey, we should scarcely have returned to Cooper's Creek at all.

After refreshment and a night's rest, they felt mildly refreshed, but it was scant compensation for the frustration in having missed the others by just a few hours. They buried some of Wills' notes and papers in the cache, and Burke wrote a brief report:

> The return party from Carpentaria, consisting of myself, Wills, and King (Gray dead), arrived here last night and found that the depot party had only started on the same day. We proceed on, to-morrow, slowly down the creek towards Adelaide by Mount Hopeless, and shall endeavour to follow Gregory's track; but we are very weak. The two camels are done up, and we shall not be able to travel faster than four or five miles a day. Gray died on the road, from exhaustion and fatigue. We have all suffered much from hunger. The provisions left here will, I think, restore our strength. We have discovered a practicable route to Carpentaria, the chief position of which lies in the 140 degrees of east longitude. There is some good country between this and the Stony Desert. From thence to the tropics the land is dry and stony. Between the Carpentaria a considerable portion is rangy, but well watered and richly grassed. We reached the shores of Carpentaria on the 11th of February, 1861. Greatly disappointed at finding the party here gone.
>
> P.S. The camels cannot travel, and we cannot walk, or we should follow the other party. We shall move very slowly down the creek.

Another bottle was found and the letter was placed inside it, this was then buried in the cache under the marked tree and King smoothed over the ground with a rake which he left lying nearby. It did not occur to them to change the mark on the tree or alter the date that Brahe had made. If Brahe, any of the others, or a rescue party were by some miraculous chance to visit Cooper's Creek again, there would be no immediate visible sign that Burke's party had ever returned from the Gulf of Carpentaria.

There was some discussion as to the route they would take next. Wills and King said they should continue behind Brahe through the desert for 150 miles, on the road back to Menindee, which was 400 miles away. Maybe something would happen to delay him, and then they would catch him up. Burke disagreed, on the grounds that if his camels and horses were in good condition, as the note (inaccurately) assured them they were, the three tired men and their two flagging camels would be no match for them. There were also long stretches on the journey without any water. Burke instead said it would be better if they went down Cooper's Creek to Mount Hopeless, where there was a police station about 150 miles away, and from there the journey to Adelaide would be through more navigable districts. The explorer Augustus Charles Gregory had already done the journey from Cooper's Creek to Mount Hopeless in a week, and the committee in Melbourne had recommended the route as a line of communication. Rather against their better instincts, Wills and King were persuaded to agree.

On the morning of 23 April they wearily resumed their march southwards from the depot, following the Cooper River downstream and then heading out into the Strzelecki Desert towards Mount Hopeless. Trying as ever to look on the bright side though morale was low, Wills was able to find some glimmers of hope as he wrote later that day:

> Having collected together all the odds and ends that seemed likely to be of use to us, in addition to provisions left in the plant, we started at 9.15 a.m., keeping down the southern bank of the creek; we only went about five miles, and camped at 11.30 on a billibong, where the feed was pretty good. We find the change of diet already making a great improvement in our spirits and strength. The weather is delightful, days agreeably warm, but the nights very chilly. The latter is more noticeable from our deficiency in clothing ...

On the next day, as they were about to start, some aborigines came past, 'from whom we were fortunate enough to get about twelve pounds of fish for a few pieces of straps and some matches, etc'. At the start of the expedition Wills had been rather condescending about the local tribes, but now he was finding them more accommodating. On 25 April they awoke at five in the morning after a good night's rest under a clear sky. As they finished breakfast:

> our friends the blacks, from whom we obtained the fish, made their appear-
> ance with a few more, and seemed inclined to go with us and keep up the
> supply. We gave them some sugar, with which they were greatly pleased – they
> are by far the most well-behaved blacks we have seen on Cooper's Creek.

Later generations might consider that for European visitors and settlers to extend goodwill by giving the aborigines food, especially flour, mutton and tea, was destructive or at least did more harm than good; it was a poor sub-stitute for their own more nutritious diet,[1] but at the time the natives were glad to be given such provisions.

After breakfast Burke, Wills and King continued in a south-westerly direction, passing across a stony point abutting on one of the largest water-holes in the creek, and struck camp soon after midday about a mile below the most dangerous part of the rocky path. One of the camels fell, but they rescued him successfully. After leaving camp in the mornings they rarely travelled more than 5 miles a day. Once again, Wills' diary serves as a rea-sonable indicator of morale on different days. Although they had had one stroke of dire misfortune after another, his optimism did not desert him altogether. Either that, or he was prepared to persevere doggedly, no matter what the future or lack of it might hold. At times one is reminded of Job in the Old Testament, plodding on resignedly despite one blow after another. His entry for 26 April was full of reassurance and hope for the future:

> Last night was beautifully calm and comparatively warm, although the sky
> was very clear. We loaded the camels by moonlight this morning, and started
> at a quarter to six: striking off to the south of the creek, we soon got on a
> native path which leaves the creek just below the stony ground and takes a
> course nearly west across a piece of open country, bounded on the south by
> sand ridges and on the north by the scrub by ground which flanks the bank
> of the creek at this part of its course. Leaving the path on our right at a dis-
> tance of three miles, we turned up a small creek, which passes down between
> some sandhills, and finding a nice patch of feed for the camels at a waterhole,
> we halted at 7.15 for breakfast. We started again at 9.50 a.m., continuing our
> westerly course along the path: we crossed to the south of the watercourse

above the water, and proceeded over the most splendid salt-bush country that one could wish to see, bounded on the left by sandhills, whilst to the right the peculiar-looking flat-topped sandstone ranges form an extensive amphitheatre, through the far side of the arena of which may be traced the dark line of creek timber. At twelve o'clock we camped in the bed of the creek at camp, our last camp on the road down from the Gulf, having taken four days to do what we then did in one. This comparative rest and the change in diet have also worked wonders, however; the leg-tied feeling is now entirely gone, and I believe that in less than a week we shall be fit to undergo any fatigue whatever. The camels are improving, and seem capable of doing all that we are likely to require of them.

Sadly, Wills spoke – or wrote – too soon. On 28 April one of the two remaining camels, Landa, became bogged in a waterhole, and it proved impossible to move him:

All the ground beneath the surface was a bottomless quicksand, through which the beast sank too rapidly for us to get bushes of timber fairly beneath him; and being of a very sluggish stupid nature he could never be got to make sufficiently strenuous efforts towards extricating himself. In the evening, as a last chance, we let the water in from the creek, so as to buoy him up and at the same time soften the ground about his legs; but it was of no avail. The brute lay quietly in it, as if he quite enjoyed his position.

They left him there overnight, but next day he had been unable to move himself. They shot him, and then cut off the edible flesh that was left. Next day they stayed where they were so they could dry the meat, although it was raining and their efforts were not very successful.

Only one camel, Rajah, was now left. On the morning of 1 May they carefully loaded him with only 'the most necessary and useful articles', carrying a small bag of bedding and clothing themselves. By next day, he was showing signs of 'being done up' and had been trembling all morning. They took pity on him by lightening his load by a few pounds, throwing out some of their sugar, ginger, tea, cocoa and two or three tin plates. On 4 May, after a bitterly cold night and morning, Rajah was so stiff he could barely get up with his load. After another two days he was 'completely done up and can scarcely get along, although he has the best of feed and is resting half his time'. Next day he was too weak to get up at all, and on 8 May he was shot when he could travel no further. Now the last of their camels was gone, Burke, Wills and King were left without proper transport or supplies; in addition, they could not carry enough water to cross the Strzelecki Desert to Mount Hopeless and so were unable to leave the creek. Their supplies were running low and they were malnourished and exhausted. Wills no longer had any of his instruments for observation or mapping, and thus little to do but write his journal up rather more fully – even if on some days there was little of importance left to say.

They could take some comfort in the fact that by this time the aborigines seemed more friendly. This was fortuitous, for with their rapidly dwindling rations they were dependent to some extent on their hospitality. Around this time, they went down the creek to reconnoitre, and found a party of them fishing. These were Cooper's Creek aborigines, members of the Yandruwandha. They gave the weary explorers about half a dozen fish each for their luncheon, and offered to share some more and a quantity of bread if they followed them to their camp. This was like manna from heaven to the explorers. Once they got to the camp, the aborigines offered them fish and a kind of bread which they called *nardoo*, a fern containing spores which could be ground into an edible flour. As the aborigines had found out through trial and error, before being eaten it needed to be soaked in water in order to get rid of the enzyme thiaminase, which would otherwise break down thiamine (vitamin B1). Not to do so would result in thiamine deficiency, which could potentially be a contributory factor to the decline in health of Burke, Wills and King. That evening, various members of the tribe came down with lumps of *nardoo* and handfuls of fish for the explorers, until they could barely eat any more. They also gave them some pieces of *bedgery*, or *pedgery*, which had a highly intoxicating effect when chewed even in small quantities, and appeared to be the dried stems and leaves of some shrub.

On 8 May Wills left Burke and King, and went on his own to look for the main channel of the Cooper, but without success. In effect, they had wasted nearly three weeks struggling down the creek. On his return, as he passed the natives' encampment, they invited him to stay the night. They offered him a place in one of their *gunyahs*, or huts, and supplied him with a much-needed meal of fish and *nardoo*, as well as a couple of 'delicious' fat rats, 'baked in their skins'. In exchange for sugar, the aborigines also gave him *padlu*, which was a type of large bean and a damper made from the ground sporocarps of the *nardoo* plant. Wills observed that some of them slept by a fire in front of the camp, and he thought them very attentive in bringing firewood and keeping the fire going throughout the night.

Meanwhile, on their return to Menindee on 29 April, Brahe had met Wright trying to reach Cooper's Creek with the supplies. Wright had lost three men, Stone, Purcell, and Becker, who all died of malnutrition. Brahe wondered whether Burke and Wills might have returned to the depot at Cooper's Creek and felt he ought to make sure. He suggested to Wright that they return and see. They set off on 3 May and were back there on Sunday, 8 May. By now, Burke and Wills were about 35 miles away from the deserted camp. As they had not altered the mark and date on the tree, Brahe and Wright assumed that Burke had not returned, and did not check the cache to see if the supplies were still buried. They noticed new footprints and the ashes of fresh campfires on the ground, but thought these had probably been made by aborigines camping there since their departure. As far as Brahe was concerned, the place still looked as it had when they had left it. They did not notice a broken bottle on top of the stockade, or a rake leaning against the tree.

They had as good as convinced themselves that they would find nothing. Having made a fifteen-minute reconnaissance sweep they were satisfied that Burke and Wills had not been back to Cooper's Creek; they remounted their animals to return south and rejoined the main party and their companions at Koorliatto Creek on 15 May.

Wills returned from his reconnaissance and overnight stay with the aborigines on 10 May to find Burke and King still cutting up Rajah into strips and laying them out in the sun to dry. Wills tried to convince Burke that the mission to try to reach Mount Hopeless was as futile as its name suggested. After being entertained by the friendly Yandruwandha, he now saw that those whom he had despised for what he called their 'primitive existence' were now their main hope. He had been fascinated watching them grind the *nardoo* into flour, but as he did not see them collect it, he was unaware that it grew on the ground and thought it must come from the trees. While Burke and King were preparing the camel flesh, Wills went to inspect the trees, but in vain. Their party was ill-equipped to live off the land; they had no hooks with which to fish and no nets with which to trap birds. Moreover, the Yandruwandha had moved further down the creek and were gone. He tried boiling the *padlu*, which could be found almost everywhere in large quantities; it boiled easily and when shelled was very sweet, tasting like French chestnuts.

The next day Burke and King started down the creek to the natives' camp, determined to find out everything they could about *nardoo*. Wills stayed behind for his turn at the meat jerking, and to try and devise some means for trapping the birds and rats, 'which is a pleasant prospect after our dashing trip to Carpentaria, having to hang about Cooper's Creek, living like the blacks'. The others returned on the morning of 12 May to report that they had been unsuccessful in their search for the locals, who had evidently moved over to the other branch of the creek. They decided to try to move out on the main creek again the next day in order to find the natives. For two more days they stayed repeating their search, but each day they came back without finding a sign of any of their new friends.

On 15 May Burke ordered the others to leave behind the last of their belongings, planning – as with the previous loads they had abandoned – to collect them at a later date, and set off again down Cooper's Creek.

Two days later, while they were following a path with the creek on their left, on approaching the foot of a sandhill, King saw some *nardoo* seeds, and they soon found that the flat was covered with them. 'This discovery caused somewhat of a revolution in our feelings, for we considered that with the knowledge of this plant we were in a position to support ourselves, even if we were destined to remain on the creek and wait for assistance from town.' What the men still did not realise was that the fern's sporocarps contained the enzyme thiaminase, which depletes the body of Vitamin B1; they were probably also not preparing the seed according to aboriginal food preparation methods. As a result, despite eating food they thought was beneficial, the men got weaker and weaker.

On 24 May, Queen Victoria's birthday, Wills and King celebrated by fetching a little more of 'what is now to us the staff of life; returned at a little after two p.m. with a fair supply, but find the collecting of the seed a slower and more troublesome process than could be desired'. While they had been picking *nardoo* in the morning, they both heard what they thought was the noise of an explosion, 'as if of a gun, at some considerable distance', and thought it must have been Burke. On their return they found that he had not been firing, and had not even heard the sound himself. It may have been the sound of a rock splitting off a distant cliff, but they thought that someone had arrived at the depot and fired a gun, maybe to attract their attention. It was decided that one of them ought to try and make the effort to return to the depot to see if anyone was there, and the choice fell on Wills.

On 27 May he set off alone, on foot, to the depot at Cooper's Creek, carrying a few days' rations, a shovel, and the diaries which he intended to bury in the cache. He found the ground thick with *nardoo* seed, and came across a group of native women with their children gathering it. They were gradually joined by several men, and they led Wills to their camp, promising him food. One man carried his shovel, another the rest of his things. He ate with them and they offered him a place in the *gunyahs* for the night, and throughout the hours of darkness they kept the fires going so that he should be warm enough.

The next day Wills did not feel well after eating some freshwater mussels, suffering constipation, but he continued on his journey and took a flock of crows fighting over a freshly killed fish by surprise. 'I decided the quarrel by taking it with me,' he wrote. 'It proved a most valuable addition to my otherwise scanty supper of *nardoo* porridge.' On 30 May, shortly before midday, he reached the depot, but found no evidence of the visit there by Brahe or others. He dug up the cache with his shovel and found it just as they had left it five weeks earlier, with Burke's letter in the otherwise empty box. To this he added another, which under the circumstances was relatively restrained but reflected something of the anger and despair he now felt:

> We have been unable to leave the creek. Both camels are dead, and our provisions are exhausted. Mr Burke and King are down the lower part of the creek. I am about to return to them, when we shall probably come up this way. We are trying to live the best way we can, like the blacks, but find it hard work. Our clothes are going to pieces fast. Send provisions and clothes as soon as possible.
> W.J. WILLS.
> The depot party having left, contrary to instructions, has put us in this fix. I have deposited some of my journals here for fear of accident.

He then shovelled the earth back and wearily returned to join the others, now without food, except for what portulac leaves he could find. Wills recorded:

> It had been a fine morning, but the sky now became overcast, and threatened to set in for steady rain; and as I felt very weak and tired, I only moved on

about a mile further, and camped in a sheltered gully under some bushes. Night clear and very cold; no wind; towards morning, sky became slightly overcast with cirrostratus clouds.

On 2 June he dragged himself into the last camp where the natives had been so kind to him on the way, but found it deserted. There were some fish bones lying around, and he gnawed at them as the only nourishment of any kind available.

Next day he had better luck. Starting at seven o'clock in the morning, after having gone about 3 miles along the south bank of the creek, he was alerted by the sound of numerous crows ahead, the sight of smoke, and a 'cooey' call from an aborigine on the opposite bank. Taking pity on the weary-looking, emaciated explorer, he directed him round the lower end of the waterhole, continually assuring him of refreshment. Wills struggled to climb up the sandy path that led to the camp, and was conducted by the chief to a fire where a large pile of fish was being cooked. These he assumed were for the general consumption of the half-dozen natives gathered around, but it turned out that they had already had their breakfast, and he was expected to eat them all himself, 'a task which, to my own astonishment, I soon accomplished, keeping two or three blacks pretty steadily at work extracting the bones for me'. Having demolished the fish, the best meal he had had for several days, next came a supply of *nardoo* cake and water until he was unable to eat any more. After being allowed a little time to digest it all, they fetched a large bowl of raw *nardoo* flour mixed to a thin paste, 'a most insinuating article, and one that they appear to esteem a great delicacy'. He was then invited to stop the night there, but he declined, keen not to overstep the bounds of accepting and presuming on their good hospitality, and with mixed feelings he took his leave. As he did so, Wills reflected on the fact that if he and the others were served generously enough by the locals at regular intervals, they would have a fair chance of surviving until the inevitable rescue party arrived, or until they were able to reach one of the larger centres of population.

On 6 June he was reunited with Burke and King, and found that in his absence they had had a couple of further severe setbacks – as if they had not had enough misfortune already. When he had left them they had been using two *gunyahs*, or huts – living and sleeping in one and using the other for storing their ammunition and supplies. Now he found Burke and King sitting in front of a burnt-out *gunyah* with their remaining possessions –

including the last of their bedding and clothing – in charred tatters on the ground. All they had left were two guns.

Burke and King had continued to barter for food with the Yandruwandha tribe, who came to give them generous bags of fish in return for items like sugar (of which they had more than they needed) and scraps of material. This proved a successful arrangement until one of the natives went into the *gunyah* where the supplies were kept, helped himself to a scrap of oil-cloth and then ran away. Burke's hasty temper got the better of him and he followed the man, firing his revolver over his head as a warning. The man dropped the cloth and took to his heels, but the incident incensed the whole tribe. The other natives invited King to come to their camp and share a meal of fish with them. He felt he could not, as Burke was not there – evidently still chasing the petty thief – and he feared that if he left the *gunyah* unguarded, he would come back later to find their supplies had been decimated behind his back. When he refused, another man took his boomerang and laid it on his shoulder, showing him in sign language that if he persisted in calling out for Burke, he would strike him. Resigned to the fact that he had nothing to lose, he followed his leader's example and fired a gun over their heads.

The aborigines had treated these last survivors of the exploring party with compassion, bringing them food on a regular basis out of kindness. When they asked for something small in return, they clearly felt Burke's ingratitude was no way to repay them. Having administered what they thought was a salutary lesson, they went away again, and late that night extended an olive branch by returning to the camp with some more cooked fish in small nets. They called out 'white fellow' and Burke went out to meet them. Angry at their apparent attempt to surround him, and probably misinterpreting their kindness, he knocked as many of the fish out of their hands as he could, and shouted out to King to fire. The shots sent them running away. King later said he thought Burke would not accept the fish because he was afraid of being too friendly with them – lest they should always be hanging around the camp – or because he resented having to offer something in exchange, and thought such bartering beneath his dignity. Had Wills been present, he might have been able to exert some moderating influence, but Burke's crass biting of the hands that, literally, fed them was another blunder which forged one more link in the chain to perdition.

A little later, Burke was cooking when a pan full of fat caught fire. A strong breeze fanned the flames, setting the *gunyah* alight. The shelter, made by the aborigines with bushes of trees, was so thickly laid that it normally served to exclude the sun and a great deal of rain. It stood no chance against the fire, and with it all their remaining possessions, except for Burke's pistol, were burnt. The Yandruwandha, who might have been their saviours if treated more diplomatically, melted away for the night, perhaps by design, or perhaps because they were going to move on anyway. With them went the last donations of food. Now there was no spare clothing, bedding, rations or food supply, except for any *nardoo* they might chance upon.

Wills had been treated with great kindness by the peoples whom he had initially despised out of traditional racial prejudice, and he was aghast when he heard what had happened. The memory of the three explorers survived for some years, and a long time later, cattlemen working in the area were told by the Yandruwandha that Burke and Wills had quarrelled violently over the episode, culminating in Wills being knocked to the ground and a stony silence existing between them as a result. Posterity only has their word for it, but the men were reaching the end of their tether, tempers were frayed, and the story is not impossible.

Determined to try and salvage what he could from this debacle, Wills started for the aborigines' camp the next afternoon in order to try and restore good relations between them. Although they had had plenty of fish to eat, they were all very weak. He himself admitted he 'could scarcely get along, although carrying the lightest swag, only about thirty pounds'. The Yandruwandha were persuaded to forgive the white men and resume deliveries of food, but the atmosphere was still tense. A couple of days later they indicated to Wills that they were moving off up the creek. The explorers were too weak to be able to keep up, and were therefore faced with having to take it in turns looking for and gathering *nardoo*, and then staying at camp grinding and pounding the seeds to eat. They still lacked the traditional knowledge to prepare it properly; they ground it without sluicing it with water and ate it raw. The natives had long since devised their own method by grinding it on the rocks so the seeds turned into flour. As the rocks had channels carved into them, they washed the powdery form down with water, reduced the resulting mixture to paste, and cooked it on the open fire. What they ended up with was a rather gritty cake with a nut-flavoured aftertaste. When eaten raw, it was like a bitter, not very pleasant type of gruel, but for Burke, Wills and King there was really no alternative.

Nineteenth-century European explorers tended to rely on stable sources of protein and carbohydrates in the form of dried meat, flour, oatmeal and rice, and they included fruit and vegetables in their diet to ensure they were consuming sufficient sources of vitamins B and C to ward off diseases such as scurvy and beriberi. When they set off from Melbourne, Burke included supplies of lime juice, preserved vegetables, dried apples and other fruits among his provisions. By the time he split the expedition and left Cooper's Creek for Carpentaria, he and his party had only a few tins of the preserved vegetables to supplement their diet of dried meat, flour, oatmeal and sugar. On their return to the creek, reduced to living on dried horse and camel flesh, they were suffering from the symptoms of vitamin B deficiency: weakness and acute pains in the back and legs.

The next few entries in Wills' diary were little more than brief notes about which of them was collecting *nardoo* and who stayed at camp to do the pounding. On 10 June they had some variation to their monotonous diet when they shot a crow. Nevertheless, for the men whose strength was gradually fading, it was an increasingly bleak existence. Five days later, Wills wrote that Burke was 'getting very weak, and I am not a bit stronger. I have determined on beginning to chew tobacco and eat less *nardoo*, in hopes that it may induce some change in the system. I have never yet recovered from the constipation, the effect of which continues to be exceedingly painful.' That same day they finished up the last of the meat that had been Rajah the camel.

On 16 June King shot another crow, but it was the nearest they got to any kind of excitement. Otherwise, over the next few days, there was basically nothing to report apart from changes in the weather, with occasional thunder, rain, and twenty-four hours later a night which was 'very boisterous and stormy; northerly wind blowing in squalls, and heavy showers of rain, with thunder in the north and west; heavy clouds moving rapidly from north to south; gradually clearing up during the morning; the wind continuing squally during the day from west and north-west'. A day after that, Wills reported that they had had an 'exceedingly cold night; sky clear, slight breeze, very chilly and changeable; very heavy dew. After sunrise, cirrostratus clouds began to pass over from west to east, gradually becoming more dense, and assuming the form of cumulostratus. The sky cleared, and it became warmer towards noon.'

Further south, meanwhile, by the beginning of June, Dr Wills was increasingly worried about his son and frustrated at the lack of any news, good or bad. On 14 June, taking only a small pack on his shoulders and a stick in his hand, he set out from Ballarat for Melbourne, stopping for a couple of nights on the way at the house of a friend, Dugald McPherson, at Bungel-Tap, before reaching his destination. Two days later he called on David Wilkie, honorary treasurer to the committee, and found him issuing circulars for a meeting to consider what action was to be taken. His heart sank when he found that nothing else had been done. He asked those he knew amongst the committee to arrange a meeting, and then went to Professor Neumayer, with reference to Mr Lockhart's letter of support, to ask if it had been arranged with Burke that a vessel should be sent round the coast to the Gulf to meet him there. The professor said that a conversation on that point had previously taken place between Burke, Wills and himself, but Burke had asked Neumayer not to move in it, for if so disposed, Burke would himself apply to the committee by letter himself.

At last the committee realised they could not sit back indefinitely and assume that silence must mean all was well, and thanks to Dr Wills' goading, they held a meeting on the evening of 18 June. Nevertheless, getting the members together was one thing, but persuading them to agree on a course of action was quite another. One after another made speeches about the expedition finances, the geography of the Australian interior and the various routes Burke might have taken.

As Dr Wills wrote afterwards, cynically, it was 'a chapter in the Circumlocution Office', and he had to intervene forcefully by impressing on them that the reason they had gathered was to send a rescue party at the earliest possible opportunity. One member asked him rather unnecessarily why he was so alarmed, and when the concerned father explained (as if any explanation was necessary) the member said dismissively that 'there was plenty of time; no news was good news', and the best thing he could do was go home and mind his own business. Fortunately there was one man there who appreciated Dr Wills' frustration. The unnamed man appealed to the committee, which almost resulted in a decision; they agreed it was time to do something, if the right people to form a rescue party were forthcoming. Dr Wills immediately volunteered, but the meeting was still adjourned.

Yet all was not lost, for the next day Secretary Dr Macadam announced that Alfred Howitt was in Melbourne and was ready to go at any time. Aged 31, Howitt had spent several years surveying and prospecting for gold. Had he put his name forward a year earlier, he would have been a prime contender for leading the expedition.[2] On 19 June the *Melbourne Argus* – an ally of Dr Wills in trying to shame the committee to take action – revealed the news that at last its members had resolved to do what the press had urged two months earlier, to send a party to Cooper's Creek in search of the expedition and its members. There was considerable discussion among the committee as to who should lead the rescue party, and even Landells was rumoured to be under consideration, but he had disgraced himself by leaving so early on. Howitt's offer did away with the necessity for Dr Wills to go, and Dr Wills returned to Ballarat, relieved that at long last something was being done.

Morale was ebbing fast among the men whom Howitt was setting out to rescue. On 20 June, after a very cold night and morning under a clear sky, Wills was suffering badly from the combined effects of cold and starvation:

> King gone out for nardoo; Mr Burke at home pounding seed; he finds himself getting very weak in the legs. King holds out by far the best; the food seems to agree with him pretty well. Finding the sun come out pretty warm towards noon, I took a sponging all over; but it seemed to do little good beyond the cleaning effects, for my weakness is so great that I could not do it with proper expedition. I cannot understand this nardoo at all – it certainly will not agree with me in any form; we are now reduced to it alone, and we manage to consume from four to five pounds per day between us; it appears to be quite indigestible, and cannot possibly be sufficiently nutritious to sustain life by itself.

Wills was so weak by the next day that he could barely crawl out of the hut, and acknowledged sadly that unless relief came in some form or other, he could not last more than a fortnight. His attitude was one of resignation tinged with bitterness at how he perceived they had been let down by the others:

> It is a great consolation, at least, in this position of ours, to know that we have done all we could, and that our deaths will rather be the result of the mismanagement of others than of any rash acts of our own. Had we come to grief elsewhere, we could only have blamed ourselves; but here we are returned to Cooper's Creek, where we had every reason to look for provisions and clothing; and yet we have to die of starvation, in spite of the explicit instructions given by Mr Burke – 'That the depot party should await our return'; and the strong recommendation to the Committee 'that we should be followed up by a party from Menindie' [sic].

By 23 June, he was too weak to crawl out of the *gunyah* at all. Burke was also visibly weakening, while King seemed to be the strongest of the three. The diary entries for the next few days betray a sense of approaching inevitable doom. They suffered 'a fearful night' on 24 June when a southerly gale sprang up before sunset and continued throughout most of the night. They found it so bitterly cold that 'it seemed as if one would be shrivelled up'. King braved the wind to go searching for *nardoo*, and returned with a satisfactory crop, but admitted that he could not keep up the work any longer, as he and Mr Burke were both rapidly getting weaker; 'we have but a slight chance of anything but starvation, unless we can get hold of some blacks'.

An event the following day rekindled Wills' old love of astronomy, although he was no longer in much of a state to enjoy it to the full:

> Near daybreak, King reported seeing a moon in the east, with a haze of light stretching up from it; he declared it to be quite as large as the moon, and not dim at the edges. I am so weak that any attempt to get a sight of it was out of the question; but I think it must have been Venus in the Zodiacal Light that he saw, with a corona around her.

On 26 June they were all losing strength, and the cold was playing 'the deuce' with them. All Wills had to keep himself warm was a 'wide-awake' hat, a merino shirt, a regatta shirt without sleeves, the remains of a pair of flannel trousers, two pairs of socks in rags and a waistcoat, of which he had 'managed to keep the pockets together'. The others were no better off than him. Apart from clothing, between them they had two small camel pads, some horsehair, 'two or three little bits of rag, and pieces of oil-cloth saved from the fire'.

The desperate situation called for some initiative, no matter how slight the chance of any success. On 27 July, after a calm night but overcast sky, an easterly breeze and bitterly cold morning, Wills suggested to Burke and King that, as the two stronger men, they ought to go further up the creek to see if they could follow the natives and bring back any more food. They were very reluctant to leave him on his own and both had to be persuaded, particularly Burke. For all his faults and hasty temper, he had become devoted to his faithful second-in-command, and hesitated to leave him to his fate, but Wills insisted, unselfishly, that it was the right thing for them to do. They told him that the very least they could do was leave him a reasonable supply of *nardoo*, water and wood for the fire to keep him going until they returned. Without it, he saw no chance of survival for any of them.

Wills was fading, slowly starving and reaching the point of no return. He kept writing up to the end, although there is some doubt as to whether his dates were always completely accurate or whether he was becoming disorientated and losing track of the calendar. Keen to leave a final message for his father, he wrote what he sensed would be a farewell letter, dated 27 June:

These are probably the last lines you will ever get from me. We are on the point of starvation, not so much from absolute want of food, but from the want of nutriment in what we can get.

Our position, although more provoking, is probably not near so disagreeable as that of poor Harry [his cousin, Lieutenant Le Vesconte, who perished with Sir John Franklin] and his companions. We have had very good luck, and made a most successful trip to Carpentaria, and back to where we had every right to consider ourselves safe, having left a depot here consisting of four men, twelve horses, and six camels. They had provisions enough to have lasted them twelve months with proper economy, and we had also every right to expect that we should have been immediately followed up from Menindie by another party with additional provisions and every necessary for forming a permanent depot at Cooper's Creek. The party we left here had special instructions not to leave until our return, unless from absolute necessity. We left the creek with nominally three months' supply, but they were reckoned at little over the rate of half rations. We calculated on having to eat some of the camels. By the greatest good luck, at every turn, we crossed to the gulf, through a good deal of fine country, almost in a straight line from here. On the other side the camels suffered considerably from wet; we had to kill and jerk one soon after starting back. We had now been out a little more than two months, and found it necessary to reduce the rations considerably; and this began to tell on all hands, but I felt it by far less than any of the others. The great scarcity and shyness of game, and our forced marches, prevented our supplying the deficiency from external sources to any great extent; but we never could have held out but for the crows and hawks, and the portulac. The latter is an excellent vegetable, and I believe secured our return to this place. We got back here in four months and four days, and found the party had left the Creek the same day, and we were not in a fit state to follow them.

I find I must close this, that it may be planted; but I will write some more, although it has not so good a chance of reaching you as this. You have great claims on the committee for their neglect. I leave you in sole charge of what is coming to me. The whole of my money I desire to leave to my sisters; other matters I pass over for the present. Adieu, my dear Father. Love to Tom [his brother who had settled in Melbourne].

P.S. I think to live about four or five days. My spirits are excellent. My religious beliefs are not in the least changed and I have not the least fear of their being so. My spirits are excellent.

When he had finished he read it aloud to Burke and King, as he felt it was important they should know that he had not written anything to which they could take offence. His diary entry, dated 29 June – although it may have been a day or two out – reported a 'beautifully warm and pleasant' day after a clear cold night, and that although Burke was suffering greatly from the cold, getting extremely weak, he and King were going to leave the next day to go up the creek to look for the natives:

I am weaker than ever, although I have a good appetite and relish the nardoo much; but it seems to give us no nutriment, and the birds here are so shy as not to be got at. Even if we got a good supply of fish, I doubt whether we could do much work on them and the nardoo alone. Nothing now but the greatest good luck can save any of us; and as for myself I may live four or five days if the weather continues warm. My pulse is at forty-eight, and very weak, and my legs and arms are nearly skin and bone. I can only look out, like Mr Micawber, 'for something to turn up;' starvation on nardoo is by no means very unpleasant, but for the weakness one feels, and the utter inability to move one's self; for as far as appetite is concerned, it gives the greatest satisfaction. Certainly fat and sugar would be more to one's taste; in fact those seem to me to be the great stand-by for one in this extraordinary continent: not that I mean to depreciate the farinaceous food; but the want of sugar and fat in all substances obtainable here is so great that they become almost valueless to us as articles of food, without the addition of something else.

Quoted as it was written with faultless spelling and punctuation, in his customary clear and steady hand, it proved to be the final entry in Wills' diary. A little later that day Burke and King went on their mission, leaving Wills with basic supplies. He watched them disappear from view as they walked along the bend in the river.

Whether he ever managed to light the fire, eat any *nardoo*, or drink the water they had left for him, nobody would know. Barring a miracle, he would now have known that they would never see each other again. There were to be no more miracles, and perhaps he was completely disorientated, or merely resigned to the inevitable – maybe both. It was fifteen months since he had written to his mother on the other side of the world, telling her that he would 'be glad to hail the chance of departing this life fairly in the execution of an honourable duty'. The hour of departure was close at hand.

As Julian Tenison-Woods, a priest and geologist who had emigrated from England to Australia, speculated in his history of exploration published four years later: maybe Wills found consolation during his last waking moments in the science which had sustained him for so long. Maybe he passed that last night, when no hope was left, deriving what comfort he could from the sight of 'the changing clouds, the fitful breezes, or the stars'.[3] Lying on his back, the surveyor would have gradually drifted into unconsciousness as his heartbeat and pulse dropped, and then into the final sleep from which there would be no awakening.

8

Aftermath

Burke and King continued upstream for another two days, taking nothing but a pistol and a few scraps of blanket. Burke was the weaker of the two, and King could see that the Irishman was nearing the end as he complained of great pain in his legs and his back. They stopped to rest for the night, and next day they continued as Burke said he thought he was getting stronger. They started once more, but after another 2 miles he said he could go no further. King tried to urge him on a little more, but could see 'that he was almost knocked up', and in desperation he threw his remaining swag away. They stopped to camp, but Burke knew that he had little time left. He gave King his watch, which he said belonged to the committee, and a pocket-book to give to Sir William Stawell, in which he wrote some notes. King shot a crow for supper, but Burke could eat very little. With his last remaining strength, Burke scrawled in his notebook the words: 'King has behaved nobly. I hope that he will be properly cared for.'

As night fell, he said to King: 'I hope that you will remain with me here until I am quite dead; it is a comfort to know that some one is by; but when I am dying it is my wish that you should place the pistol in my right hand, and that you leave me unburied as I lie.' Early next morning he was unconscious, and at around daybreak, like his second-in-command before him, he slipped peacefully into death.

King spent a few hours sitting by the body, and then stayed there for a couple of days, resting until he felt a little stronger, living off his small stock of *nardoo*. At night he slept in deserted huts. After a couple of days he found some huts where the natives had left a large quantity of *nardoo*, he shot a few crows, then made his way back to where they had left Wills, only to find him lying dead in the *gunyah*. The natives had been there and taken some of his clothes. He covered him with sand, the best burial he could provide in view of his own failing strength. Now he was completely on his own.

As the precise date on which both explorers died could not be ascertained, different dates are given on various memorials throughout Victoria, but the Exploration Committee fixed on 28 June 1861. While starvation and exposure were partly responsible, their deaths may have also been caused by thiamine deficiency, or beriberi – one of the symptoms of which was the leg and back pain Burke had complained of in his last few days.

Incongruously, the long-discussed relief party had just set out on its way to meet the explorers. Led by Alfred Howitt, it comprised Edwin Welch, a surveyor, and two assistants, Alex Aitkin and Weston Phillips. They left on 26 June, having decided to go to Menindee and make their way up to Cooper's Creek via 'Burke's track'. Three days later they met Brahe on his way down to Melbourne. As soon as he heard Brahe's news, Howitt realised that a more substantial expedition would need to be assembled if Burke and Wills were to be found, and he contacted the committee in Melbourne to say that he and Brahe were returning immediately. They were back on 30 June and reported all they knew to Sir Henry Barkly and Sir William Stawell of the committee at Government House. The news was: four men were dead; Wright's party was back at Menindee; Wright himself had gone to Adelaide; Burke and Wills were missing since 16 December and presumed somewhere, alive or dead, in the north.

Secretary Dr Macadam assembled the other committee members, and they gathered in the Royal Society of Victoria's rooms in the afternoon. Now the committee felt a little guilty at not having moved earlier, and were apprehensive as to what the press would say when they heard the news. Brahe was questioned as to why he had left Cooper's Creek before his provisions were exhausted: why had he not made any effort to communicate, or sent a message to Menindee; or kept a diary; did he have any idea as to where Burke and Wills were now? Though he was unable to answer the most important questions, he acquitted himself well enough, and was asked to write up a diary of events from memory and from the rough notes which he had made.

Howitt then suggested that he set out a second time, with a rather larger party than before. Brahe offered to come with him as his experience would be invaluable. The committee prevaricated, decided a subcommittee should be formed to make arrangements, and then adjourned for the night. Next day they came to a decision and agreed that Howitt should have a free hand in taking as many people as he thought fit, then starting as soon as possible. His party was ready on 4 July, containing Brahe and seven others. All the Australian colonies had been roused by the news of the missing explorers, and simultaneous offers to help were forthcoming from all directions.

As they set out on their way, news began to reach Melbourne that all was not well. On 5 July the *Melbourne Weekly Age* published an article under the heading 'THE NEWS FROM THE EXPLORING EXPEDITION'. The 'unexpected news', it told its readers, was 'positively disastrous', with its members 'dissipated out of being, like dewdrops before the sun'. In a report of about 1,200 words, it mentioned that some were dead, though it only named 'poor Becker', who 'had scarcely the physique for encountering the toils of such an expedition in particular'. It inferred that he was probably not the only casualty, although what had become of Burke and Wills was still anyone's guess, and advocated sending out a search party without delay in order to rescue anybody who might have survived – even if it was too late. It emphasised that the most important thing to be done now was for the committee to try and save the rest of the party by sending an enlarged relief force. The whole expedition, it said, appeared to have been:

one prolonged blunder throughout; and it is to be hoped that the rescuing party may not be mismanaged and retarded in the same way as the unfortunate original expedition was. The savans [savants – learned scholars, in this case a derogatory reference to the committee] have made a sad mess of the whole affair; let them, if possible, retrieve themselves in this its last sad phase.[2]

Howitt and his men made excellent progress, with the advantage of travelling during the best time of year, and they found water at almost every halt. On 13 September they rode into the depot at Cooper's Creek, and Brahe said it looked to him exactly as it had when he last returned in May, with nothing to indicate that anybody apart from the natives had been there. Yet they did not think to open the cache, and stayed there only a few minutes, camping several miles down the creek.

Next day they reached the place at the creek where Burke's party had camped for the last time before heading north for the Gulf of Carpentaria. At last they could see evidence of recent visits, in the form of camel droppings and tracks in places where Brahe was sure Burke's camels had not been on the outward journey. Howitt was convinced that stray camels must have been there in the last four months.

On 15 September they went a few miles further, and a close examination of the ground revealed further camel and horse footprints. Yet the greatest discovery of all came from Welch, who had been alerted by the natives to a solitary, pathetic-looking figure clad in rags and part of a hat. 'He presented a melancholy appearance,' Howitt recorded, 'wasted to a shadow, and hardly to be distinguished as a civilised human being by the remnant of clothes upon him.'[3] Welch asked the man his name, and was astonished when he answered weakly that he was King, the last survivor of the expedition – and that Burke and Wills had long since died. Burnt by the sun, and suffering from malnutrition, he was carried to the camp. Dr Wheeler of the rescue party said that he would certainly have died within a few days if he had not been found. At first he was so disorientated that the others noticed he seemed to be having difficulty in following what they said, but after a light meal of rice and other supplies, and the first comfortable night's rest for a very long time, he appeared a little better.

Howitt sat beside him with a notebook and pencil, writing down his story as he told them bit by bit what had happened. It was partly from this testimony and partly from Wills' field books, which would be recovered later that week, that the sad story gradually emerged. King had been given Burke's pocket book and Wills' farewell letter to his father, and he handed them to Howitt. The latter secretly feared as he jotted everything down that there was the possibility King might collapse and die before he had finished telling the story, but fortunately such fears were not realised.

King began by telling of the deaths of Burke and Wills, and of his struggle to stay alive when they had not. He had shot a few more birds, and the noise of his gun had brought the tribesmen out to meet him. They seemed to understand that he was alone, cooked the birds for him, and gave him shelter and *nardoo*. As they wanted to know where Burke lay, one day when they were fishing in the waterholes nearby, he led them to the place. When they saw the body, they wept bitterly, and then collected sprays from the bushes with which to cover it, as a mark of respect. After that, King felt, they sensed his loneliness even more, and redoubled their kindness to him, looking on him as one of their own. This state of affairs continued for about a month, until one day, one of the men who had been fishing came to tell him that the 'white fellows', Howitt's party, were on their way.

After another couple of days, King was well enough to lead Howitt and the rest of the party to Wills' grave, 7 miles down the creek. Sadly, the native dogs had been there first and the body was horribly mangled, with hardly anything left of the skull except for the lower jaw. The men gathered up the remains, and also dug up his remaining diaries from nearby. Welch removed some of Wills' hair from the camel cushions on which he lay when he died, and to the 'regret and sorrow' of Dr Wills, on his return to Melbourne Welch gave some of these fragments to his friends as keepsakes.

Although King was exhausted when they returned to camp that night, a few days later he managed to explain to them where Burke's body was lying. On 21 September Dr Wheeler remained in camp with King, while the others went to find the place. The dingoes had been scavenging there as well, and the hands and feet were missing. His revolver, corroded with rust, still cocked and capped, lay a few feet away, leading to suspicions that Burke may have meant to shoot himself if he had been a little stronger. They placed his remains in a Union Jack and lowered them into a new grave. Once more, the souvenir-hunting Welch took some of the hair, cutting off fragments with a penknife.[4]

By 25 September, Wheeler decided King was strong enough to travel. They set off along the creek, reaching the Cooper's Creek depot three days later. Here they dug up the cache containing the field books, Burke's letter, Wills' final note and a few other notebooks. King had to be treated very carefully, riding on his horse and stopping regularly for rest. His mood proved very changeable; sometimes he was cheerful and talked to the others as he rode, at other times he was dull and unresponsive, totally self-absorbed. On 11 October Brahe and one of the other men were sent on ahead to break the news to the rest of the world.

The sorry truth about relations between the three British men on the expedition and the natives with whom they came into contact was con-firmed over a century later by a great-grandson of one of the Yandruwandha people on Cooper's Creek. He said that William John Wills, whom they knew as 'Wiltja', was 'a good fellow', always trying to make gestures of friendship towards them, and was accordingly made welcome by them in return. John King was likewise 'a decent man', and seemed to them 'like a woman, because he was always seen to be doing things for the others, more or less waiting on them'.[5] Burke's insistence on discouraging them from being too accommodating or friendly proved their undoing, and as he had resorted to violence on two occasions, the natives kept their distance, watching from afar until King was seen to be alone. Wills was seen as friendly, and if Burke had listened to him when advised to maintain good relations with 'the blacks', they would probably all have still been alive when Alfred Howitt's rescue party arrived three months later. The kind-hearted Yandruwandha were moved to tears when they saw the corpses of Burke and Wills. If only Burke had been persuaded by the others to see reason, instead of treating the natives as thieving savages to be warned off at every available opportunity, it might have all been so different.

A man named James Wills – who was probably no relation but had been a servant at Ashburton Grammar School when William John Wills was there – had settled with his wife in Victoria. While the press was alive with questions as to what had happened to the ill-fated explorers, he and Mrs Wills were walking on the banks of the Murray when she caught sight of two unfamiliar-looking animals on the distant horizon. She insisted that they were camels, but her husband told her she must be mistaken, as no such animals were to be found in the wild in Australia. Convinced that they could be nothing else, she walked towards them and found that she was right. More fortunate than some of the other beasts which had ended up on dinner plates, they had escaped from the expedition – almost certainly the pair that Wills and McDonough had lost the previous November – and sniffed water from a distance. When Mrs Wills carefully offered them some food, the younger one came up and ate gently out of her hand. Mr Wills informed the police, who forwarded the information to the Governor of Victoria, Exploration Committee member Sir Henry Barkly.

Back at Melbourne, on 19 September, Dr Wills was summoned to Major Egerton Warburton's office to receive the news that there were rumours of a sighting of what was believed to be the missing party. Some white men were living on a raft on a lake, naked, supporting themselves by catching fish, and had camels nearby. He was sure that one of the men must be his son. But it proved to be a false alarm. Nothing more was heard until 2 November, after Brahe had returned to Melbourne. That night Dr Wills was staying with friends who had gone out to the opera, yet they returned home unexpectedly early. A servant came to say that he wanted to speak with him privately, and had to break the terrible news which he had been dreading. His son and Burke were dead. Nobody on the committee had yet been informed. Dr Wills subsequently had the sad duty of informing Dr David Wilkie, the committee treasurer, and Dr Macadam the committee secretary.

The rescue party had meanwhile brought King back to Melbourne; he was to be totally bewildered by the crowds that awaited him and cheered as he entered the city in the last week of November. The man who had been spared by providence to become the sole survivor of the expedition to Carpentaria was greeted as a celebrity; the nineteenth-century equivalent of a teenage idol. Yet he was still very lethargic, had barely recovered from his ordeal, and visibly shrank from those who wanted not only a sight of him but also to touch him, or even try and snip off a lock of his hair as a souvenir.

When the train they were on drew up at the North Melbourne station, King and Welch were to be transferred to an open carriage for a reception before the Royal Society committee members, the Governor of Victoria and political leaders of Victoria. Dr Wills felt that as the bereaved father of one of those who had not returned, he was being slighted by not being invited. As the train stopped, he forced his way into the compartment, greeted King emotionally, seized him by the arm and tried to take him out of the carriage. He declared that he was acting as the representative of the committee and had been given instructions to take King directly to Sir Henry Barkly, the Governor of Victoria. Welch told him firmly that he had his orders to take King to Spencer Street Station where Dr Macadam was waiting for them both. An angry Dr Wills told him in no uncertain terms that he was flouting Sir Henry Barkly's express wishes, but Welch would not be cowed, and a fuming Dr Wills had no alternative but to stay in the compartment and accompany them both to their destination.

The train pulled in to a huge outburst of cheering, and the waiting crowds gathered round so closely that the porters could not open the doors. At length Welch forced his way out, leading an utterly bewildered King with Dr Wills in hot pursuit. He hailed a cab and all three got inside, heading for Government House. More crowds had assembled outside the Royal Society's premises, but when they saw King and his escorts going in a different direction, they ran, rode or commandeered the nearest carriage to follow. At Government House, King, uncomfortable with being the focus of attention and now shaking with terror, was taken to the chief secretary's office. His sister and Governor Sir Henry Barkly, who had had to force their way in through the throng which was now swarming all over the building, joined him and Welch. Keen to assert his right to be there, Dr Wills had made his way in through a side door as well. Barkly realised that King was still very frail after his ordeal and experiences, and that nothing more could be expected of him at the moment. Once the noise had died down, his sister took him back to her house for a long-overdue rest and total quiet.

Soon after King's return, Wills' watch, a gold chronometer, which he had used to calculate the longitudes, was delivered to his father in Barkly's presence. It was accompanied by his last letter from Cooper's Creek, dated 27 June 1861. Distinctly traced in a firm hand on a ruled page torn from a notebook, it was unsealed and neatly wrapped in a loose cover. With its restrained but critical remarks about the shortcomings of the other parties, and in particular its scathing verdict regarding 'great claims on the committee for their neglect', Dr Wills promptly released the letter to the press. He prudently omitted the postscript which referred to his son's religious views being unchanged, as he felt it would do William's reputation no good if the people of Victoria felt that their unlucky explorer was a resolute atheist.

Back in Totnes, Mrs Wills received a telegram and letter from Sir Henry Barkly, dated 26 November, in which he sent his deepest sympathies and those of the entire local community on her son's death. He assured her that she could 'rely upon it that the name of William John Wills will go down to posterity, both at home and in this colony, amongst the brightest of those who have sacrificed their lives for the advancement of scientific knowledge and the good of their fellow-creatures'.

Earlier that same week, on 22 November, a Royal Commission of Inquiry into the failure of the expedition and the deaths of Burke and Wills was opened – it sat at twelve separate meetings over the ensuing nine weeks. No reference was made to the other five men who had perished, and the terms of reference included the rather loaded phrase: 'to investigate the circumstances under which the depot at Cooper's Creek was abandoned by William Brahe'. Sir Henry Barkly, in his capacity as President of the Royal Society, as well as Governor of Victoria, appointed the board's five commissioners. Three were local politicians, while the chairman, Major-General Sir Thomas Pratt, was Barkly's father-in-law. Only one, Francis Sturt, a police magistrate, could be said to have any knowledge of exploration; he was the brother of the explorer Charles Sturt. On behalf of the Royal Society,

Dr Macadam was the first witness to be summoned. He said that it had never been the committee's intention that Burke should divide his party at Menindee, but rather that the full company should reach Cooper's Creek. Instead he had vanished, going ahead with Wright and a small party to Cooper's Creek.

Brahe was then summoned to give evidence, and although he had been criticised in the press for apparently deserting his post at the depot, he acquitted himself well. The question which could never be satisfactorily answered was whether he was being truthful when he said Burke had told him to remain only three months at the depot. The only person who might have been able to do so, McDonough, was called next, but he denied having heard any instructions to that effect. It was apparent that Burke had not left written instructions to anybody during the expedition, only his notes towards the end, saying he had expected to find Brahe at his post when returning to Cooper's Creek in April. King was called next, and as he was still suffering mentally in the aftermath of his ordeal, the commissioners treated him gently. Brahe and Wright were then questioned again, and although there were attempts to cast them as the guilty men responsible for the deaths of the leaders, Burke's vagueness in his verbal orders to others and his general plans, having left no paper trail, made it impossible to apportion blame.

The Commission published its report in January 1862. It censured Burke for having 'most injudiciously divided' the expedition, 'having been provided and equipped in the most ample and liberal manner', after reaching Menindee without difficulties; and, notwithstanding the sudden resignations of Landells and Beckler, for his error of judgement in appointing Wright to an important command in the expedition without any knowledge of him or his abilities. It was said that Burke had 'evinced a far greater amount of zeal than prudence' in departing from Cooper's Creek before the depot party had arrived from Menindee, without communicating with the other relevant parties, contrary to his instructions, and 'overtaxing the powers of his party' by undertaking such an extended journey with inadequate provisions. Moreover, he had neglected his duties by disregarding the committee's advice, failing to keep a regular journal and give written instructions to his officers. Had he done so, 'many of the calamities of the expedition might have been averted'. Wright's conduct in delaying his departure for so long without adequate explanation was 'reprehensible in the highest degree'. Brahe was censured for 'retiring from his position at the depot' before being rejoined by his commander. Nevertheless, there were mitigating factors in that 'responsibility far beyond his expectations had devolved upon him'. He had, after all, remained at Cooper's Creek for longer than he believed had been agreed, and Patton's severe illness had justified his not staying on indefinitely. The Exploration Committee had committed 'errors of a serious nature' in overlooking the contents of Burke's despatch from Torowoto Swamp written in October 1860, and in not urging Wright's departure from Menindee more quickly.

Justice was thus seen to have been done. Dr Wills, however, thought that Brahe should have been reproved more thoroughly. There was briefly speculation that criminal proceedings ought to be taken against Wright for negligence, but such an action was never likely to succeed. Nevertheless, he was regarded by many as the guilty man, with a reputation he was never likely to live down, and he retired to obscurity in Adelaide.

On 24 July 1862 John McDouall Stuart, who had led the rival expedition from Adelaide, reached the ocean on the northern coast at Darwin Bay. He had been seventeen months behind Burke and Wills in traversing Australia from north to south. It was the sixth of his expeditions across the subcontinent, and the third in which he had attempted to complete the crossing from north to south. He never lost a single man during any of them, but by the time he returned to Adelaide he was in poor health, and at one stage his men did not expect him to survive. After trying to resume his surveying career, he returned to London in 1865 in poverty, to be cared for by a sister until his death the following year.

Now that one chapter had in effect been closed, it was felt that the government must do what it could to make amends for the untimely loss of the men who had carried so heavy a burden. It was decided that the leaders should be given a public funeral, and a monument should be erected in their memory. Late in 1862 Howitt was given instructions by the committee to return to Cooper's Creek to disinter and bring back what remained of the bones of Burke and Wills. Howitt collected all the remains he could find, re-wrapped both sets in a Union Jack, and placed them in boxes which were loaded onto camels. He took them first to Adelaide and then by steamer to Melbourne, where they arrived in December and were taken to the Royal Society Hall.

On New Year's Eve 1862, the society held a formal ceremony of 'coffining' the bones. They were about to unlock the metal boxes when it was discovered that the only key was in the possession of Dr Macadam, who was not present. The audience were impatient for proceedings to take place, and several other keys were tried but in vain. Just as members were about to take a crowbar to the boxes, Dr Macadam staggered in, explaining that he had been overcome with a sudden disposition as he was very upset. Next day the press reported tersely that he was drunk. Now the ceremony could proceed, and the bones which had been recovered were carefully laid out on sheets, ready for burial. Wills was sadly incomplete, the vertebrae and skeleton kept together by the remains of the shirt in which he died. These bones included a small amount of his beard, 'sufficient in itself to prove the identity of the remains'. Eager to obtain a few mementoes of the grue-some occasion, some members of the committee helped themselves to a few teeth, locks of hair and other parts of the explorers' mortal remains. It was said that in the months to come, such relics would be passed around at dinner parties as a conversation piece.[6]

The bodies of Burke and Wills were laid in state for two weeks, and it was estimated that over 100,000 people filed past to see them. On 21 January 1863 they received a state funeral. Shops and offices throughout Melbourne closed for the day, a public holiday was declared, and about 40,000 people, or three-quarters of the city's population, turned out to line the streets and watch the procession. The funeral car was a replica of the one in which the body of the Duke of Wellington had been taken to his grave in St Paul's Cathedral some ten years earlier. Six plumed black horses led the carriage with decorated wheels and an open canopy above the coffins, while Tom Wills and John King were among the pallbearers.

Dr Wills, who had returned to England the previous summer, did not return to Australia for the occasion. The burial service of the Church of England was read, but there was neither any music nor funeral oration. Afterwards, as the procession reached the cemetery, spectators gathered around, anxious to see the mortal remains of the two men, and the pallbear-ers had to push their way towards the grave. Police had to clear the crowd back to a respectful distance before Burke and Wills were lowered into the grave and buried side by side; a firing party from the police guard stepped forward and fired three shots as a mark of respect.

A public fund was opened for a monument, and the government voted £4,000. The sculptor Charles Summers produced a vast work with out-size figures – Burke standing 12ft high, his right hand resting on the shoulder of Wills, who is sitting beside him holding the diary in his hand.

A granite pedestal below had four bronze bas-reliefs showing the start of the expedition, the return to Cooper's Creek, the natives lamenting the death of Burke, and the discovery of King. It was completed in 1864 and erected on the hill at the corner of Collins Street and Russell Street, in the centre of Melbourne. In 1886, due to increased traffic in the area, it was moved to a new site outside Parliament House where it remains to this day. Other memorials and plaques were erected throughout Victoria and Queensland.

In Totnes, people were quick to honour the memory of William John Wills. At a public meeting in January 1862 he was unanimously acclaimed as the most distinguished member of the 'Wills and Burke' (not Burke and Wills) expedition. His maps, journals and notes would be invaluable to posterity and to future settlers, in contrast to the superficial notes left by Burke and the 'vague and uninteresting' recollections of King. In August 1864 a granite obelisk, funded by contributions from Totnes townsmen and those from Devon who had settled in Australia, was erected at The Plains, in Totnes, alongside the house where William and his siblings had been born. In 1892 Mr Angel, who had returned to Totnes on a visit from South Australia, where he too had emigrated some thirty or forty years before, found that the inscription on the memorial was becoming obliterated, and he provided funds for it to be renewed on a tablet of white marble set into the granite. A large medallion bearing Wills' profile, executed by Mr F. Horn, a local mason, was added to the memorial a year later.

A memorial of a different kind was provided when the botanist Dr Ferdinand Mueller named a newly discovered Australian plant *Eremophila Willsii*, otherwise known as the sandhill native fuchsia, which has an attractive purple flower. The act was 'to record by botany the glory never to be forgotten of the intrepid and talented but most unfortunate Wills', in memory of the fact that it was 'only by his guidance and scientific talents' that the great geographic success of the expedition was achieved.[7]

John King went to live quietly with his sister, Mrs Bunting, a wardress at the Melbourne Lunatic Asylum in St Kilda, one of the city's suburbs. He married his cousin Mary in 1872, but he never completely recovered from his ordeal, and it was thought that even at the time of the expedition he may have been suffering from tuberculosis. Nevertheless, he survived for nearly twelve years before succumbing in 1873, aged 34, and was buried, appropriately, in the city cemetery beside the two men with whom he had endured such hardship. In 1863 he had been granted a pension by the government of £180 a year, but this ceased at his death and his widow, his wife of just one year, received nothing.

One potentially unpleasant discovery was made by a rescue party which had set out from Adelaide in mid-August 1861 to search for Burke and Wills. John McKinlay and his deputy William Hodgkinson – who had formerly been part of Burke's party – led a party of five men from Gawler, north of Adelaide. On 20 October they were close to Cooper's Creek when a group of natives guided them to a waterhole, where they found a couple of graves. One body, dressed in a flannel shirt with short sleeves, was clearly a European man, probably British. The skull bore evidence of what looked like two sabre cuts. When the news reached Melbourne, there was speculation that it must have been Charley Gray, and that while already ill he had been attacked by Burke with a shovel, thus hastening his death. It was suggested that the severed head and lack of flesh on the body might have been the work of animal scavengers, or – a far worse possibility – of Burke, Wills and King removing some prior to burying him in order to supplement their depleted rations. Had this been the case, it was certainly something Wills would never have dared to mention in his diary. Alternatively, the corpse may not have been Gray at all, but instead an unfortunate member of some other expedition, or an unlucky settler who had lost his way.

Burke was posthumously awarded a gold medal by the Royal Geographical Society in London for his achievements. As only one medal could be awarded for any particular expedition, Wills was accorded no similar honour, while King was presented with a gold watch.

The Victorian government voted £2,090 as a bequest to Mrs Wills in Devon, and £500 each for his two sisters, in addition to a grant of £150 to Dr Wills to cover his journey back to England. He resigned from his appointment of surgeon superintendent, and left Australia on 18 June 1862 on board *Cairngorm*. Later that year he published his son's account of the venture with extensive quotations from his letters and diaries, in what was in effect a biography, under the somewhat ironic title *A Successful Exploration through the Interior of Australia*. The book has remained an invaluable record of the doomed enterprise, although written with understandable bias. To quote Alan Moorehead, 'either by innuendo or outright denunciation he demolished nearly everybody's reputation'.[8] Surprisingly, Dr Wills' writings treated Burke gently, but Wright, Brahe, Landells, Becker and others were all taken to task, and of Dr Macadam, secretary of the committee which he felt had so much to answer for, he sincerely trusted that 'it may never be my fortune to come in contact with him again in any official business whatsoever'.

Two years later, Dr Wills spent a short time in New Zealand as a ship's surgeon on the immigrant ship *Lancashire Witch*, arriving in Auckland in June 1865 – but he was back in England the following year. By 1869 he and Sarah were living at Ethelmead, Cleveland Road, Torquay. Sarah died in 1880 and he outlived her by nine years, dying on 2 February 1889, both at Marldon. They were buried there at St John the Baptist Church.

It has been claimed that Dr Wills fathered three illegitimate children during his time in Australia and that his housekeeper, May McDonald, was the mother. They were raised, so the story goes, by a Mr and Mrs Luckhurst in Tasmania, and were given their mother's surname in order to avoid any scandal.

William's brother Tom, who had shared the journey to Australia in 1852, found employment on the railways, and worked his way up to become the station master at Ballarat. He married Anne MacDonald and they had a son, appropriately named William John in his uncle's memory, born at Gisborne, Victoria, in 1868. William John the younger married Martha Alice Smith in 1889 and they had six children including two sons, one also named William John and another Robert O'Hara Burke. Tom died at Ballarat on 20 May 1909, and his first son, William John, on 25 September 1946. Several of their descendants still live in Victoria.

Their other brother Charles, the 'Charley' whose reading lists and home-work Wills had so meticulously tried to plan from the other side of the world, became a bank clerk in Totnes, and died unmarried on 8 September 1864, fifteen days short of his twenty-fifth birthday. Of the sisters, Elizabeth Margaret (Bessy) married Humphrey Joseph Hare, while Hannah lived and died a spinster.

Robert Watson, another Devonian who had settled in Victoria at about the time of the gold rush, was among those who wrote tributes to Wills which were published in the *Totnes Times* in November 1861. He penned his in verse:

> Your hero has passed to no ignoble grave;
> He died not 'ere a deathless fame was won;
> And earth must count amongst her true and brave,
> The brave and patient Wills, Devonia's son.

Successive writers have observed that, human nature being what it is, had Burke and Wills returned to the depot twenty-four hours earlier in April 1861, and thus been saved from their fate, posterity would have taken much less interest in them than it has in the men who literally died for their cause. As a result of the tragedy at Cooper's Creek, 'they were lifted to another and a higher plane, one might even say a state of grace'.[9]

Although the expedition had ended in tragedy for both its leaders, it had not been an unmitigated failure, and there were several who maintained that it had been a success. It had been the first to cross the continent from sea to sea, and had thus fulfilled the mission on which it had been sent forth in the interests of science and civilisation. G.C. Leech, a barrister from Castlemaine, argued that no Briton would deny that the battle of Trafalgar had been any the less a glorious victory because Nelson was killed at the scene, and in fact it was Burke and Wills' success, not their failure, that had cost them their lives.[10]

'Seldom has human fortitude and endurance been put to a severer test than the disappointment which awaited them,' wrote *The Times* in its initial report at the end of the expedition:

> He perished, indeed, as it is probable that Franklin perished, through a series of mishaps which a heathen would have ascribed to the malice of fortune, but, like him, he accomplished the main object of his mission, and, unlike him, he opened new fields to civilized man, which settlement, following close on the track of discovery, will soon rescue from desolation.[11]

Although the correspondent was referring to Burke, the words are equally applicable to his deputy. When the official inquiry into the expedition criticised various aspects of the venture, among them Burke's leadership, they could not find a word to say against Wills. He was rightly seen as modest, trustworthy and studious; widely regarded as a faithful second. It might hardly be overstating the case to call him the principal victim, the one who might have saved himself and the others if his judgement had been allowed to prevail.

Burke had proved himself a strong, decisive leader, with the ability to inspire affection and devotion in his men. Yet as a personality he was too impetuous, impatient and obstinate, lacked organisational skills and was ill-prepared by temperament to take advice from others and admit that sometimes they might be right. As the expedition leader he was fatally flawed. Notwithstanding the natural diffidence of his second-in-command, with hindsight the man who would almost certainly have been a better, wiser and less headstrong commander was William John Wills. Those who had known him personally said that he never complained to others, never blamed others for things that went wrong (except in his writings, a personal safety net, when any mortal had every right to feel aggrieved), and proved unswervingly loyal to his leader.

Opinion is divided as to how the expedition might have fared with Wills in charge. In retrospection, some have suggested that had he been appointed leader in the first place, history might have had a happier tale to tell. If he had not been a victim of the mistakes of others, perishing all alone at the age of 27, he would instead have returned to Melbourne safe and well. In the years afterwards he would almost certainly have risen to the top of his profession as a surveyor, or become a leading figure in the annals of Australian science.

While his diaries and letters revealed a certain amount of what he did and thought during his short life and those increasingly hopeless last few weeks, an air of mystery remains over his tragic fate, as with so many others who have perished down the ages alone and far from home. What thoughts ran through his mind as he lay dying but still conscious, resigned to the inevitable end? He and Burke had completed their overland crossing, but failed to live long enough to reap the benefits. Did he resent being denied his chance to bask in the heroes' welcome in which he should have shared on returning to Melbourne? Did he wish that he had been permitted to take responsibility for some of the major decisions, which he would have been perfectly capable of making? Had it been otherwise, his would have been a much happier fate.

Notes

The majority of references and quotations in the text, including all in Chapter 1, 'A Devon Childhood', and Chapter 6, 'Return to Cooper's Creek', are taken from Dr William Wills, *A Successful Exploration through the Interior of Australia* (London: Richard Bentley, 1863). The list below comprises those taken from other sources.

2 Early Life in Australia

1 Angela Thirlwell, *Into the frame: The four loves of Ford Madox Brown* (London: Chatto & Windus, 2010), p. 57
2 T.W. Windeatt, 'Wills, the Australian explorer', *Report and Transactions of the Devonshire Association*, XXV, p. 390
3 Ibid.
4 R.W. Vanderkiste, *Lost – but not for ever: My personal narrative of starvation and providence in the Australian mountain regions* (London: James Nisbet, 1863), p. 9
5 Tim Bonyhady, *Burke and Wills: From Melbourne to myth* (Balmain: David Ell Press, 1991), p. 49

3 Exploration

1 Bonyhady, *Burke and Wills*, p. 30
2 Ibid., pp. 41–2
3 Sarah Murgatroyd, *The Dig Tree: The extraordinary story of the ill-fated Burke and Wills expedition* (London: Bloomsbury, 2002), p. 82
4 Bonyhady, *Burke and Wills*, p. 50
5 Murgatroyd, *The Dig Tree*, p. 72

4 The Beginning of the Expedition

1 Bonyhady, *Burke and Wills*, p. 89
2 Ibid., p. 110
3 Ibid., p. 108
4 Ibid.

5 From Cooper's Creek to Carpentaria

1 Murgatroyd, *The Dig Tree*, p. 158
2 Ibid., p. 204
3 Alan Moorehead, *Cooper's Creek* (London: Hamish Hamilton, 1963), p. 79
4 Ibid., p. 80; Murgatroyd, *The Dig Tree*, p. 12

7 Into the Final Sleep

1 John Rickard, *Australia: A cultural history*, 2nd edition (London: Longman, 1996), p. 59
2 Murgatroyd, *The Dig Tree*, p. 277
3 Julian Tenison-Woods, *A history of the discovery and exploration of Australia*, Vol 2 (London: Sampson Low, 1865), p. 377

8 Aftermath

1 John King narrative; *Illustrated London News*, 1 February 1862
2 *Melbourne Weekly Age*, 5 July 1861
3 *Alfred Howitt Journal*, 15 September 1861; *Illustrated London News*, 1 February 1862
4 Bonyhady, *Burke and Wills* (exhibition catalogue, 2002), p. 1

5 Private information from Wills' family
6 Murgatroyd, *The Dig Tree*, p. 333
7 Windeatt, 'Wills, the Australian explorer', p. 402
8 Moorehead, *Cooper's Creek*, pp. 125–6
9 Ibid., p. 209
10 Bonyhady, *Burke and Wills*, pp. 198–9
11 *The Times*, 17 February 1862

Bibliography

Books

Bonyhady, Tim, *Burke and Wills: From Melbourne to myth* (Balmain: David Ell
Press, 1991)

———, *Burke and Wills: From Melbourne to myth* (exhibition catalogue)
(Canberra: National Library of Australia, 2002)

Clune, Frank, *Dig: A drama of central Australia* (Sydney: Angus and Robertson,
1937)

Jackson, Andrew, *Robert O'Hara Burke and the Australian exploring expedition of 1860*
(London: Smith, Elder, 1862)

Moorehead, Alan, *Cooper's Creek* (London: Hamish Hamilton, 1963)

Murgatroyd, Sarah, *The Dig Tree: The extraordinary story of the ill-fated Burke and
Wills expedition* (London: Bloomsbury, 2002)

Newnham, W.H., *Melbourne: The Biography of a City* (Melbourne: F.W. Cheshire,
1956)

Rickard, John, *Australia: A cultural history*, 2nd edition (London: Longman, 1996)

Russell, Percy, *The good town of Totnes* (Exeter: Devonshire Association for the
Advancement of Science, 1964)

Tenison-Woods, Julian, *A history of the discovery and exploration of Australia*,
2 volumes (London: Sampson Low, 1865)

Thirlwell, Angela, *Into the frame: The four loves of Ford Madox Brown* (London: Chatto & Windus, 2010)

Tipping, Marjorie, *Ludwig Becker: Artist and naturalist with the Burke and Wills expedition* (Carlton: Melbourne University Press, 1979)

Vanderkiste, R.W., *Lost – but not for ever: My personal narrative of starvation and providence in the Australian mountain regions* (London: James Nisbet, 1863)

Wills, Dr William, *A Successful Exploration through the Interior of Australia* (London: Richard Bentley, 1863)

Articles and Conference Papers

McKellar, John, 'William John Wills', *Victorian Historical Magazine*, 2 February 1962, pp. 337–50

Sullivan, Pamela, Notes from a talk given to the Burke and Wills Historical Society Conference, April 2009

Windeatt, T.W., 'Wills, the Australian explorer', *Report and Transactions of the Devonshire Association*, XXV, pp. 389–405, read at Torquay, 1893

Other Sources

Illustrated London News
Oxford Dictionary of National Biography
The Times
Burke and Wills website: www.burkeandwills.net.au

Index